TEXTS FROM CHRISTIAN LATE ANTIQUITY

Volume 1

The Wisdom of St. Isaac of Nineveh

The Wisdom of
St. Isaac of Nineveh

SEBASTIAN P. BROCK

GORGIAS PRESS
2006

First Gorgias Press Edition, 2006.

Copyright © 2006 by Gorgias Press LLC.

ISBN 1-59333-335-8

This publication has been made possible by a generous grant from

Deacon Gabriel Can

GORGIAS PRESS
46 Orris Ave., Piscataway, NJ 08854 USA
www.gorgiaspress.com

Printed and bound in the United States of America.

CONTENTS

INTRODUCTION

St Isaac of Nineveh, or St Isaac the Syrian (as he is often known), is a figure full of paradox: a hermit of the Assyrian Church of the East who lived in the seventh century, he is in the present century, through his writings which have been translated into a dozen or more different languages, perhaps more influential than at any other time in history: on Mount Athos his works remain favourite monastic reading, and in Egypt their inspiration lies behind the monastic revival in the Coptic Orthodox Church during the last few decades. Through modern translations into English, French and Italian, his writings have also become known to, and appreciated by, many outside the monastic circles for which St Isaac originally intended them.

Reactions to his teaching, however, have not always been favourable: in some quarters within his own Church objection was taken, not long after his death, to certain aspects of his teaching, and in the present century one eminent scholar dismissed his writings with the words 'we see in him a milestone on the melancholy road whereby the Orient lapsed from Christianity into an unprogressive, uninventive barbarism, in which not even philosophy continued to flourish'.[1] Yet for many people today St Isaac clearly does have the ability to speak directly, over the span of thirteen centuries. Eloquent testimony to this is given by a young Greek Orthodox monk, whose words are quoted by Archimandrite Vasileios, of Stavronikita Monastery on Athos:[2]

> I am reading St Isaac the Syrian. I find something true, heroic, spiritual in him; something which transcends space and time. I feel that here, for the first time, is a voice which resonates in the deepest parts of my being, hitherto closed and unknown to me. Although he is so far

---

[1] F. C. Burkitt, at the conclusion of his review of the English translation by A. J. Wensinck, in the *Journal of Theological Studies* 26 (1924/5), p. 86.

[2] Archimandrite Vasileios, *Hymn of Entry. Liturgy and Life in the Orthodox Church* (St Vladimir's Seminary Press, Crestwood, 1984), pp. 131-2.

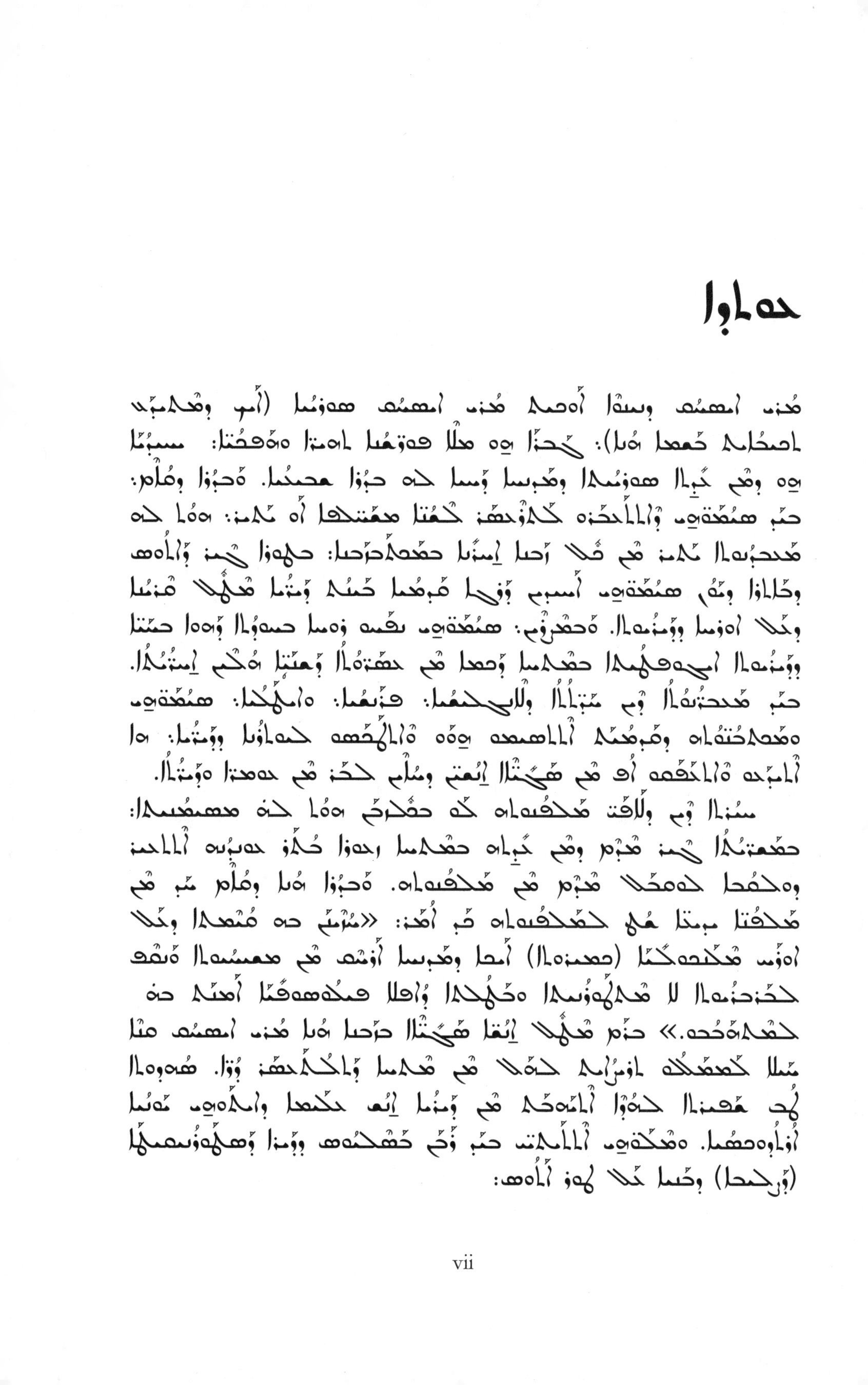

removed from me in time and space, he has come right into the house of my soul. In a moment of quiet he has spoken to me, sat down beside me. Although I have read so many other things, although I have met so many other people, and though today there are others living around me, no one else has been so discerning. To no one else have I opened the door of my soul in this way. Or to put it better, no one else has shown me in such a brotherly, friendly way that, within myself, within human nature, there is such a door, a door which opens onto a space which is open and unlimited. and no one else has told me this unexpected and ineffable truth, that the whole of this inner world belongs to man.

Little is known of the circumstances of St Isaac's life. Like a number of other distinguished Syriac writers of the seventh century, St Isaac was born in the region of modern Qatar, on the Gulf, and it must have been there that he received his early monastic training and education, when he will have first become familiar with the great writers on the spiritual life, both Syriac and Greek (in Syriac translation), men such as St Ephrem, John the Solitary, Evagrius, Macarius, Abba Isaiah, Mark the Monk and many others.

The only fixed chronological point in his life was his consecration as bishop of Nineveh (Mosul) by George, who was Catholicos Patriarch of the Church of the East from 661-681. St Isaac's episcopal career, however, was a brief one since, 'for a reason which only God knows' (as one biographical notice put it) after only five months in office he retired to live the life of a hermit somewhere in the mountains of southeast Iraq, attached to the monastery of Rabban Shabur. There he appears to have lived to an old age, and it was perhaps only then that, at the urging of his spiritual disciples, he committed his teaching on so many different aspects of the spiritual life to writing.

In the form in which they have been transmitted St Isaac's surviving works fall into a 'First Part' and a 'Second Part'. The First Part, which consists of 82 homilies, had a wide circulation, and was already by the eighth/ninth century read in monastic circles of Churches other than his own, for it was approximately then that most of this collection of homilies was translated into Greek in the Orthodox monastery of St Saba, in Palestine. Incorporated into this translation, and given under St Isaac's name, are five texts which are not in fact by him: four of these are by another, slightly later, monastic writer of the Church of the East, John the Elder (also known as John Saba, or John of Dalyatha), while the fifth is an

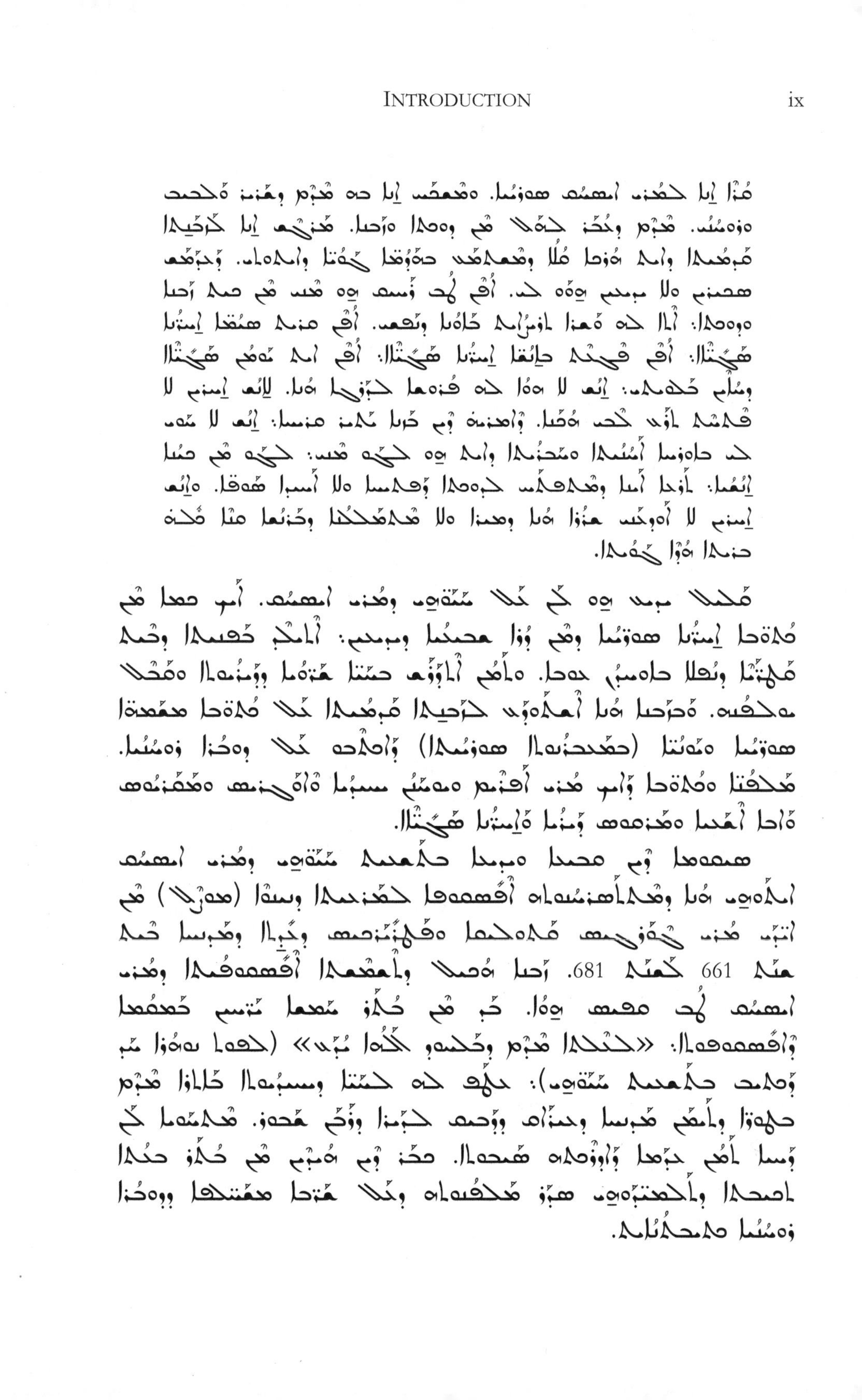

abbreviated form of a letter on the spiritual life by the Syrian Orthodox theologian Philoxenus of Mabbug, who died in 523.

In the course of the Middle Ages translations from this Greek version were made into Georgian, Arabic (and thence Ethiopic), Latin and Slavonic (some other translations into Arabic were made direct from Syriac). By the early sixteenth century St Isaac had also been translated into Portuguese, Catalan, Spanish, French and Italian. Although the Latin translation was printed a number of times in the sixteenth century, it was not until 1770 that the Greek text was first published in printed form, edited by the monk Nikiphoros Theotokis. It is this Greek text (unfortunately based on late and poor manuscripts) that has served as the basis for most subsequent translations—into Romanian (1781), Russian (1854; and thence into Japanese, 1910), Modern Greek (1871), French (1981) and English (1984)— and for the various modern reprints of the Greek. Although considerable excerpts from St Isaac's writings were included in the eleventh-century monastic anthology compiled by Paul Evergetinos, nothing by him features in the better known *Philokalia*, edited by St Nikodimos of the Holy Mountain in 1782, only a dozen years after the appearance of the printed edition of the Greek text of St Isaac. This absence, however, has been remedied in the Russian (1884) and Romanian (1981) editions of the *Philokalia*, and it was from the former that the English translation of a selection of texts by St Isaac in *The Early Fathers from the Philokalia* (1954) derives. It was not until 1909 that the Syriac original of the First Part was published in full, by Father Paul Bedjan, an indefatigable editor of Syriac texts, and it was from this that the standard English translation by the Dutch scholar A. J. Wensinck was made (1923).

The existence of the Second Part was already known to Bedjan who, at the end of his edition of the complete Syriac text of the First Part, gave a few extracts of this Second Part from an old manuscript in Urmia (northwest Iran), regretting at the same time that he could not give more, 'car il s'y trouve de fort belles pages'. Although this manuscript evidently shared in the dismal fate of the Christian population of Urmia in 1918, a little over two decades earlier, in 1896, the Reverend Yaroo Neesan,[3] a native Christian of the Urmia area in American Episcopalian orders who

---

[3] Information concerning Neesan can be found in J. F. Coakley, 'Yaroo M. Neesan, "A missionary to his own people"', *Aram* 5 (1993), pp. 87-100, and more briefly in his *The Church of the East and the Church of England: a History of the Archbishop of Canterbury's Assyrian Mission* (Oxford, 1992), p. 118-20.

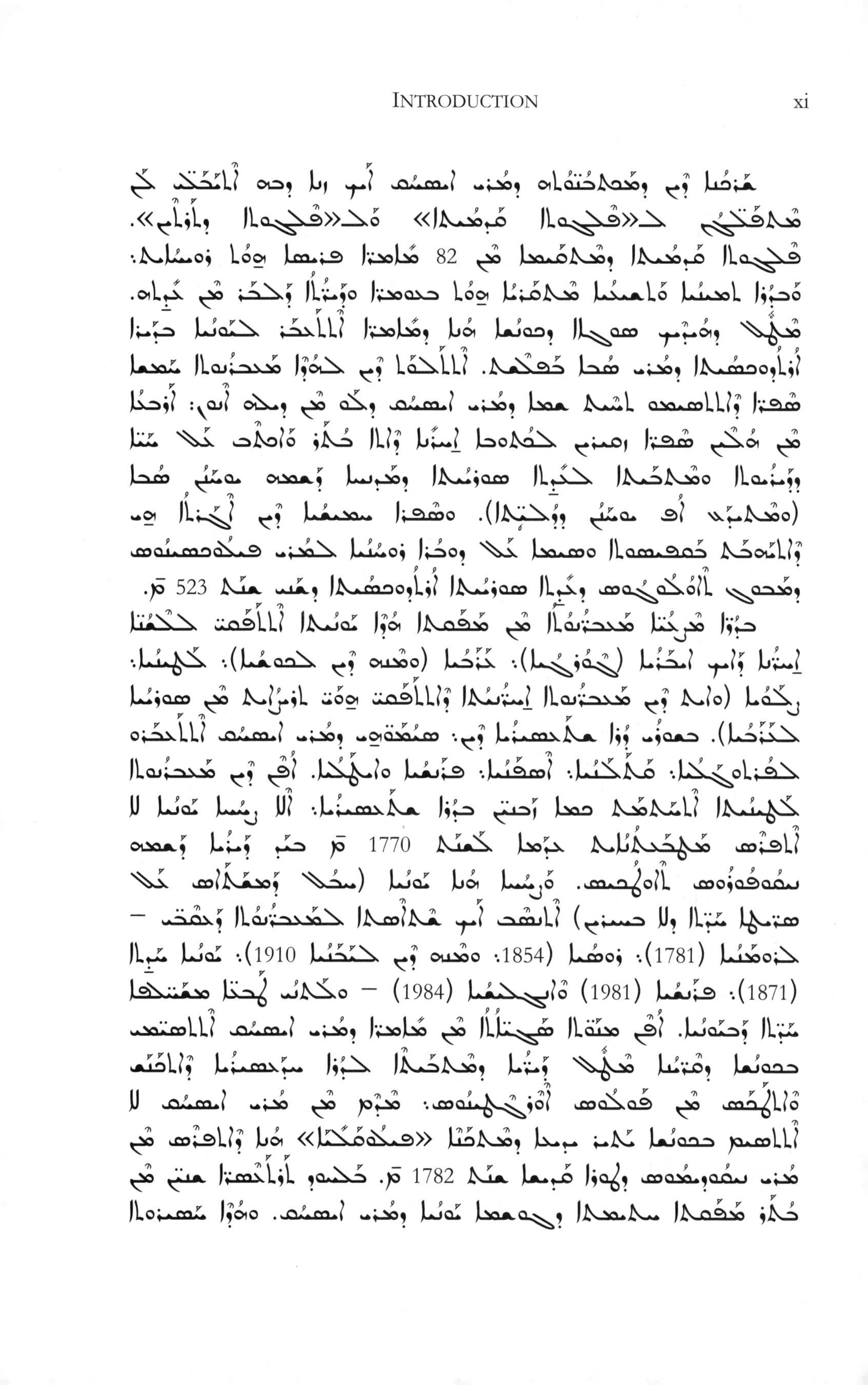

was working for the Archbishop of Canterbury's educational mission to the Assyrian Church of the East (based in Urmia), had fortunately sold to the Bodleian Library in Oxford another old manuscript of what has turned out to be the same work. The precise identity and significance of this manuscript, however, was not recognized until nearly a century later, and so these new homilies are only now in the process of being published and translated.

Although the Second Part was never translated into Greek, it was nevertheless read in Syriac in Orthodox circles, since extracts from it survive in a few old Melkite Syriac manuscripts in the library of St Catherine's Monastery, Sinai, and elsewhere. At least parts of it also circulated in Arabic translation.

The Second Part consists of a collection of 41 texts, of which the third is by far the longest, being in fact a group of four series of 'Kephalaia', or 'Headings', consisting of mostly fairly short sayings on the topic of spiritual knowledge. Attention to one particular of these sayings, which happened to have been among the extracts from the Second Part selected by Bedjan at the end of his edition of the First Part, was long ago drawn by Irenée Hausherr; it deserves quoting in full here:[4]

> If zeal had been appropriate for putting humanity right, why did God the Word clothe Himself in the body in order to bring the world back to His Father, using gentleness and humility? And why was He stretched out on the cross for the sake of sinners, handing over His sacred body to suffering on behalf of the world? I myself say that God did all this for no other reason except to make known to the world the love that He has, His aim being that we, as a result of our greater love arising from an awareness of this, might be captivated by His love when He provided the occasion of this manifestation of the Kingdom of heaven's power—which consists in love—by means of the death of His Son.

The whole tenor of St Isaac's approach here to the history of salvation, with its emphasis on the love of God, aptly anticipates one of the most striking chapters in the Second Part, devoted to the topic of the mystery of Gehenna; in this he forcefully argues that the conception of Gehenna

---

[4] I. Hausherr, 'Un précurseur de la théorie scotiste sur la fin de l'Incarnation', *Recherches de science religieuse* 22 (1932), pp. 316-20, reprinted in his *Études de spiritualité orientale* (Orientalia Christiana Analecta 183; 1969), pp. 1-5.

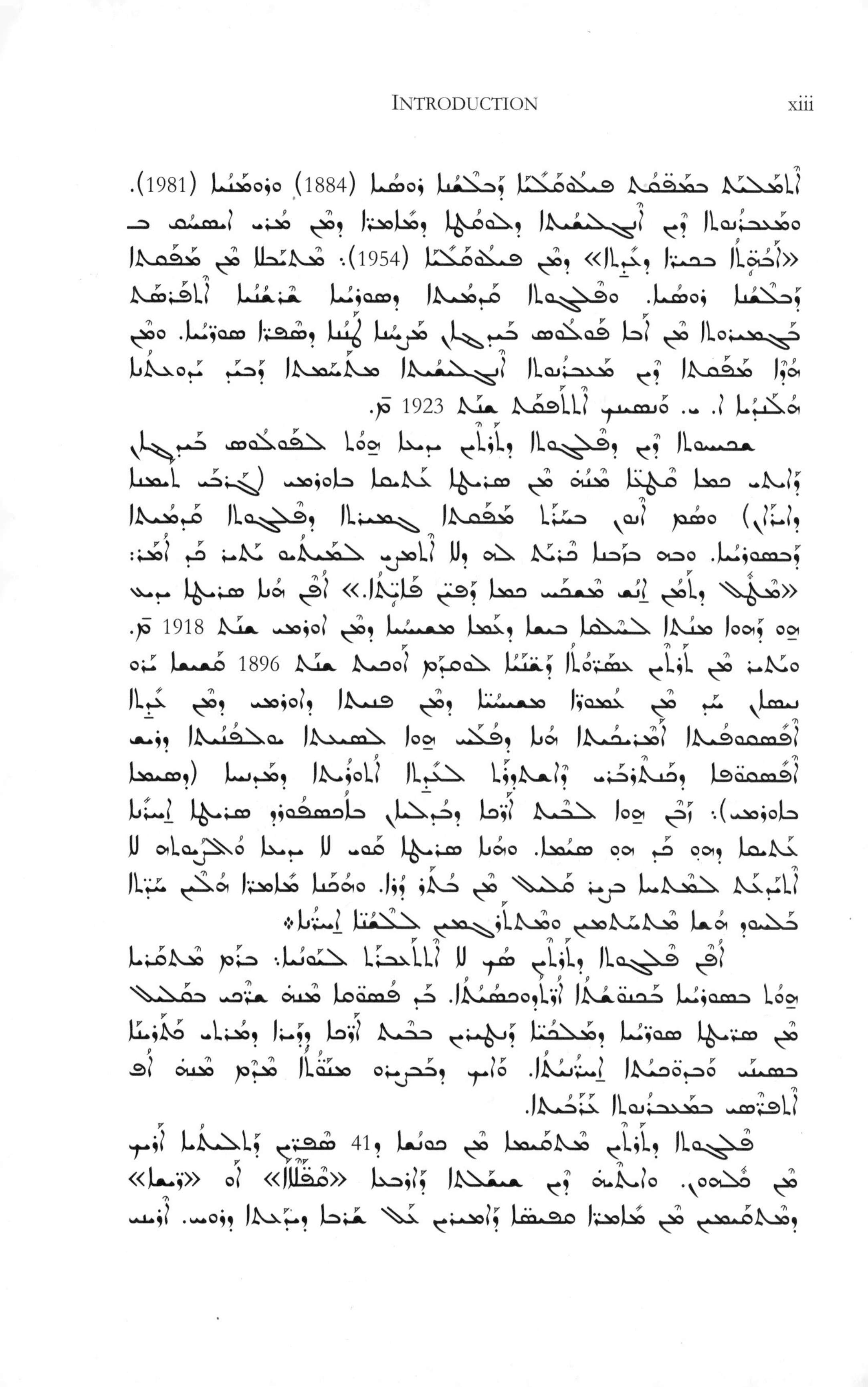

envisaged as consisting in eternal or retributive punishment is totally incompatible with any true understanding of God's love and providence; St Isaac's own view is that

> ... even in the matter of the afflictions and sentence of Gehenna there is some hidden mystery, whereby the wise Maker has taken as a starting point for its future outcome the wickedness of our actions and our wilfulness, using this as a way of bringing to perfection His dispensation ... which lies hidden from both angels and human beings, and is hidden too from those who are being chastised, whether they be demons or human beings, hidden, that is, for as long as the ordained period of time holds sway.

And a few paragraphs further on:

> That we should say or think that the matter of Gehenna is not in reality full of love and mingled with compassion would be an opinion full of blasphemy and insult to our Lord God. By saying that He will even hand us over to burning for the sake of sufferings, torment and all sorts of ills, we are attributing to the divine Nature an enmity towards the very rational beings which He created through grace; the same is true if we say that He acts or thinks with spite and with a vengeful purpose, as though He was avenging Himself. Among all His actions there is none that is not entirely a matter of mercy, love and compassion: this constitutes the beginning and end of His dealings with us.[5]

Finally, mention should be made of a Third Part which has recently come to light in a late manuscript in Tehran. Of this there is already an Italian translation, and a French translation is shortly to appear.

*

The present selection of 153 short sayings by St Isaac is drawn from both the First and the Second Part, and it follows the sequence of these two volumes. References are given in an abbreviated form, as follows: for the First Part, homily/chapter number in Wensinck's translation of the Syriac text + page number in Bedjan's edition (indicated in the margin of Wensinck's translation); for the Second Part, homily/chapter + section number, except in the case of the Kephalaia where the series (I-IV) +

---

[5] Chapter 39.

number within the series is given. For convenience, a short index of topics is provided at the end.

The first edition of *The Wisdom of St Isaac* was published in Kottayam (Kerala, India) by the St Ephrem Ecumenical Research Institute (SEERI) in 1995 (with a shorter introduction); a second edition, with the present introduction, was published by the SLG Press (Convent of the Incarnation, Fairacres, Oxford) in 1997, and reprinted in 1999; there are also Dutch, German and Arabic translations.[6] This third edition updates the bibliography and provides the Syriac text. I am most grateful to the Revd Dr Jacob Thekeparambil, Director of SEERI, and to the SLG Press for their gracious permission to reprint the translation and introduction, to Raban Awgen Aydin for the Syriac translation of the introduction, to Revd Deacon Gabriel Can for the generous grant supporting this publication, and to Dr George Kiraz of Gorgias Press for the idea, and realization of, this bilingual edition.

Sebastian Brock

---

[6] Arabic tr. 1998; Dutch tr. by Annabelle Parker, in *Qolo Suryoyo* 136 (2002), pp. 95-122; German tr. by Karl Pinggéra, *Die Weisheit Isaaks des Syrers* (Würzburg: Der Christliche Osten, 2003).

*

((SEERI)
SLG (:
SEERI
_SLG

FOR FURTHER READING: MAIN EDITIONS AND TRANSLATIONS OF ST ISAAC

FIRST PART
(a) Syriac text

P. Bedjan, *Mar Isaacus Ninivita, de Perfectione Religiosa* (Paris/ Leipzig, 1909).

(b) Complete translations (82 chapters)

A. J. Wensinck, *Mystic Treatises by Isaac of Nineveh* (Amsterdam, 1923; reprinted Wiesbaden, 1969). [From Syriac].

[D. Miller], *The Ascetical Homilies of Saint Isaac the Syrian, translated by the Holy Transfiguration Monastery* (Boston, 1984). [From the Greek translation; contains an excellent introduction. It should be noted that the order of chapters in the Greek is quite different from that of the Syriac; a useful concordance can be found in this   volume].

J. Touraille, *Isaac le Syrien. Oeuvres spirituelles* (Paris, 1981). [From Greek].

(c) Selections

E. Kadloubovsky and G. E. H. Palmer, *Early Fathers from the Philokalia* (London, 1954), pp. 183-280. [Excerpts translated from the Russian Philokalia].

S. P. Brock, *The Syriac Fathers on Prayer and the Spiritual Life* (Kalamazoo, 1987), pp. 242-301. [First Part, ch. 22; Second Part, ch. 14-15; and short extracts from both Parts].

M. Hansbury, *St Isaac of Nineveh, On Ascetical Life* (Crestwood NY, 1989). [Ch. 1-6].

A. M. Allchin, *The Heart of Compassion* (London, 1989; Japanese translation, 1990). [60 short excerpts].

M. Gallo and P. Bettiolo, *Isacco di Ninive: Discorsi ascetici* (Rome, 1984). [Ch. 1-38].

S. Chialà, *Isacco di Ninive. Un'umile speranza. Antologia* (Communità di Bose, 1999). [Includes some texts from the Second Part].

INTRODUCTION

SECOND PART
(a) Syriac text

S. P. Brock, *Isaac of Nineveh (Isaac the Syrian). 'The Second Part', Chapters IV-XLI* (Corpus Scriptorum Christianorum Orientalium, Scr. Syri 224-5; Leuven, 1995). [The English translation is in Scr. Syri 225].

(b) Complete translations (41 chapters)

A. Louf, *Isaac le Syrien. Oeuvres spirituelles - II. 41 Discours récemment découverts* (Spiritualité Orientale 81; Abbaye de Bellefontaine, 2003).

Ioan I. Ica Jr, *Isaac Sirul. Cuvinte catre singuratici. Partea II recent descoperita* (Sibiu, [Romania], 2003).

(c) Selections

P. Bettiolo, *Isacco di Ninive. Discorsi spirituali. Capitoli sulla conoscenza, Preghiere, Contemplazione sull'argomento della gehenna, Altri opuscoli* (Communità di Bose, 1985, enlarged second edition, 1990). [This includes Ch. I-III, not yet published in Syriac]

H. Alfeyev, *Prepodobnij Isaak Sirini* (Moscow, 1998).

Ch. 1-2: S. P. Brock, 'Two unpublished texts by St Isaac the Syrian', *Sobornost/Eastern Churches Review* 19 (1997).

Ch. 1-3: P. Bettiolo [see (b)].

Ch. 4-41: S. P. Brock [see (b)].

Ch. 4-5: N. Nin (tr.) and S. Chialà (introd.), *Isaac de Níneve, Centúries sobre el coneixement* (Clàssics del Cristianisme 99; Barcelona, 2005).

Ch. 5: S. P. Brock, 'The prayers of St Isaac the Syrian', *Sobornost/ Eastern Churches Review* 16 (1994), pp. 20-31.

THIRD PART

S. Chialà, *Isacco di Ninive. Discorsi ascetici, terza collezione* (Communità di Bose, 2004).

A. Louf, [French translation forthcoming].

STUDIES

H. Alfeyev, *The Spiritual World of Isaac the Syrian* (Cistercian Studies Series 175; Kalamazoo, 2000). [There is a French translation of the slightly larger Russian edition (Moscow, 1998) by A. Louf, *L'Univers spirituel d'Isaac le Syrien* (Spiritualité orientale 76; Abbaye de Bellefontaine, 2001).

S. Chialà, *Dall'ascesi eremitica alla misericordia infinita. Ricerche su Isacco di Ninive e la sua fortuna* (Florence, 2002).

S. P. Brock, 'From Qatar to Tokyo, by way of Mar Saba: the translations of Isaac of Beth Qatraye', *Aram* 11/12 (1999/2000), 275-84.

_____, 'Syriac into Greek at Mar Saba: the translation of St Isaac the Syrian', in J. Patrich (ed.), *The Sabaite Heritage in the Orthodox Church from the Fifth Century to the Present Day* (Orientalia Lovaniensia Analecta 98; Leuven, 2001), pp. 2001-8.

_____, 'Isaac the Syrian', in G. and V. Conticello (eds), *La théologie byzantine*, I (forthcoming).

TEXT AND TRANSLATION

THE WISDOM OF SAINT ISAAC

1. The ladder to the Kingdom is hidden within you, and within your soul. Dive down into your self, away from sin, and there you will find the steps by which you can ascend up.

    [Hom. 2, B 12]

2. Do not test out your mind on the grounds that you are examining what seductive and impure thoughts look like, imagining that, as you do this, you will not be overcome by them. Even the wise have in this way been thrown into confusion and become infatuated.

    [Hom. 2, B 14]

3. Do not be inept in the requests you make to God, otherwise you will insult God through your ignorance.

    [Hom. 3, B 32]

4. When someone asks a human prince for a load of dung, not only will that person be despised as a result of his despicable request, but he has also offered an insult to the prince by means of his stupid request. Exactly the same applies when someone asks for the things of the body in prayer.

    [Hom. 3, B 32]

5. If God is slow in answering your request, or if you ask but do not promptly receive anything, do not be upset, for you are not wiser than God.

    [Hom. 3, B 33]

6. Anything that is easily found is also easily lost, whereas what is found after much labour will be guarded with vigilance.

    [Hom. 3, B 34]

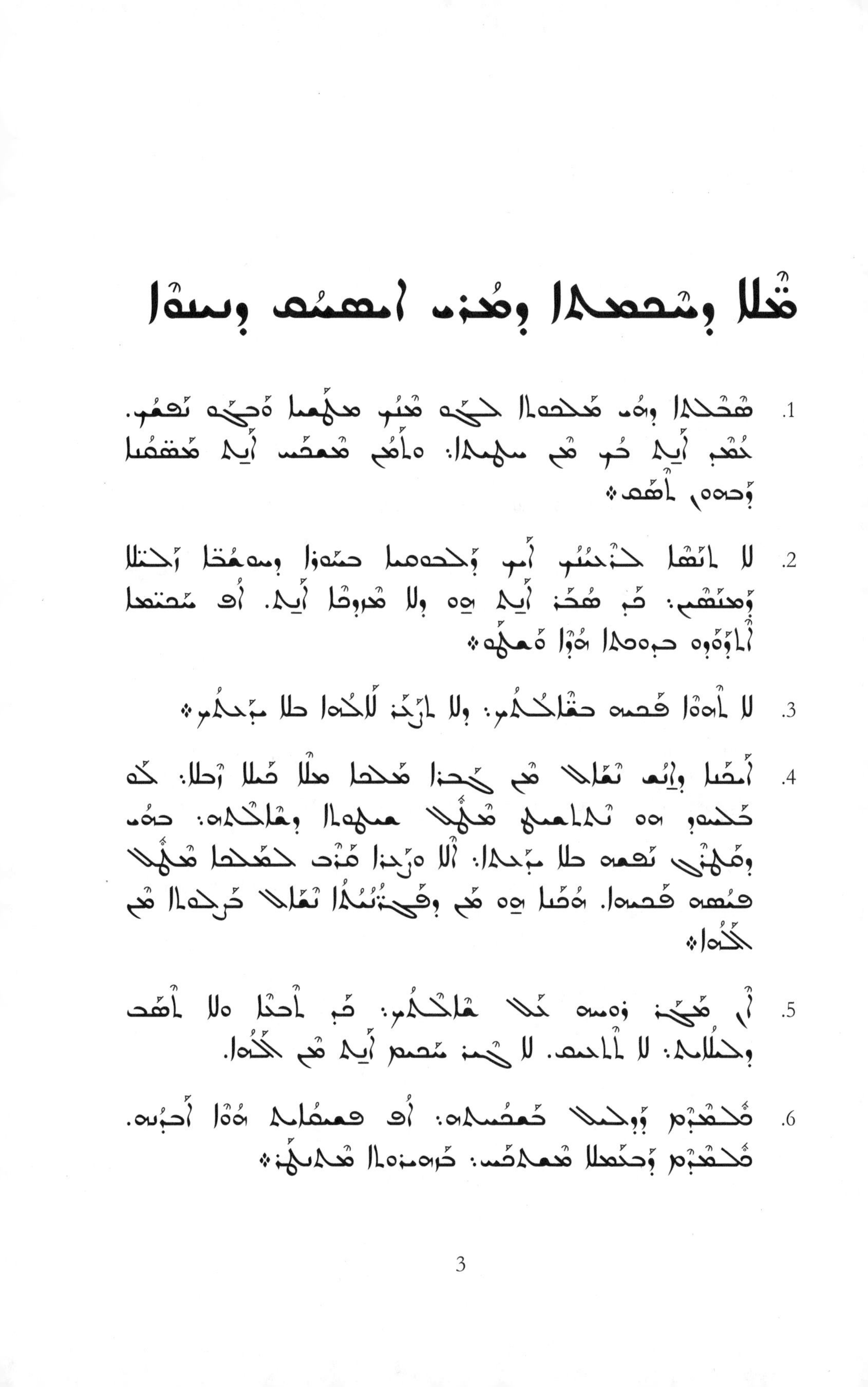

3

7.   Thirst for Jesus, so that He may inebriate you with His love.

[Hom. 3, B 34]

8.   Without temptations, God's concern is not perceived, nor is freedom of speech with him acquired, nor is spiritual wisdom learnt, nor does the love of God become grounded in the soul.

[Hom. 3, B 36]

9.   Make sure you see to small things, lest otherwise you may push aside important ones.

[Hom. 4, B 44]

10.   A full stomach abhors examining spiritual matters, just as a prostitute dislikes talking about chastity.

[Hom. 4, B 53]

11.   Fire will not catch alight with wet wood, and fervour for God will not be kindled in a heart that loves ease.

[Hom. 4, B 54]

12.   When the Evil One sees a person commence on some virtuous action with great fervour of faith, he has the habit of placing grievous temptations in that person's path, so that the love in their mind is blunted and they are frightened away from this course of action.

[Hom. 5, B 61-2]

13.   If you owe God a small coin over some matter, He is not going to accept from you a pearl in its place.

[Hom. 5, B 63]

14.   Divine care surrounds all human beings all the time, but it is only seen by those who have purified themselves from sins and who have God in mind at every moment.

[Hom.5, B 64]

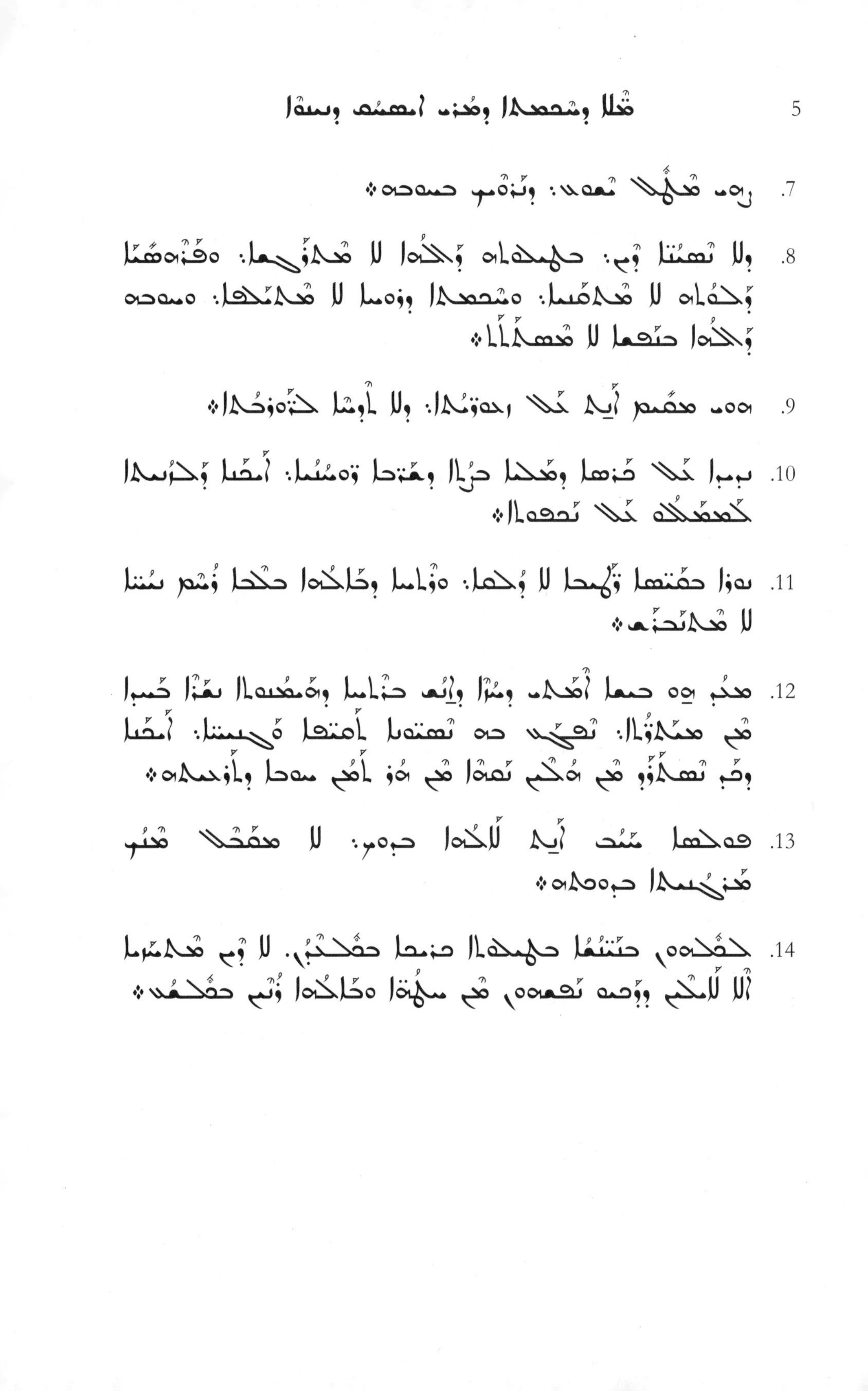

15. If you believe firmly that God cares for you, then you do not need to worry about the body, nor need you be concerned about discovering ways how to conduct your life. If, however, you doubt God's care, and want to look after yourself without God, then you are the most miserable person imaginable.

[Hom. 5, B 67]

16. The person who benefits the poor finds that God takes care of him.

[Hom. 5, B 68]

17. When you are ill, say "Blessed are those who discover the purpose set by God in the things that God brings upon us for our advantage. God is bringing this sickness for the sake of the soul's good health".

[Hom. 5, B 69]

18. Before you fall ill, search out a doctor for yourself. Before difficulties come upon you, pray; then, when the time of distress comes, you will discover prayer, and it will provide an answer for you.

[Hom. 5, B 75]

19. The heart of the Lord is directed towards the humble, to benefit them. The face of the Lord is set against the proud, so as to humble them. Humility receives compassion continuously, whereas a hard heart and absence of faith continually meet with unexpected difficulties.

[Hom. 5, B 76]

20. Do not feel loathing for any horrible illnesses of the sick, for you too are clothed in flesh.

[Hom. 5, B 78]

21. Love sinners, but reject their deeds. Do not despise them because of their failings, lest you too find yourself tempted in the very same way. Remember that you too share in the stink of Adam, and that you too are clothed in this same weakness.

[Hom. 5, B 79]

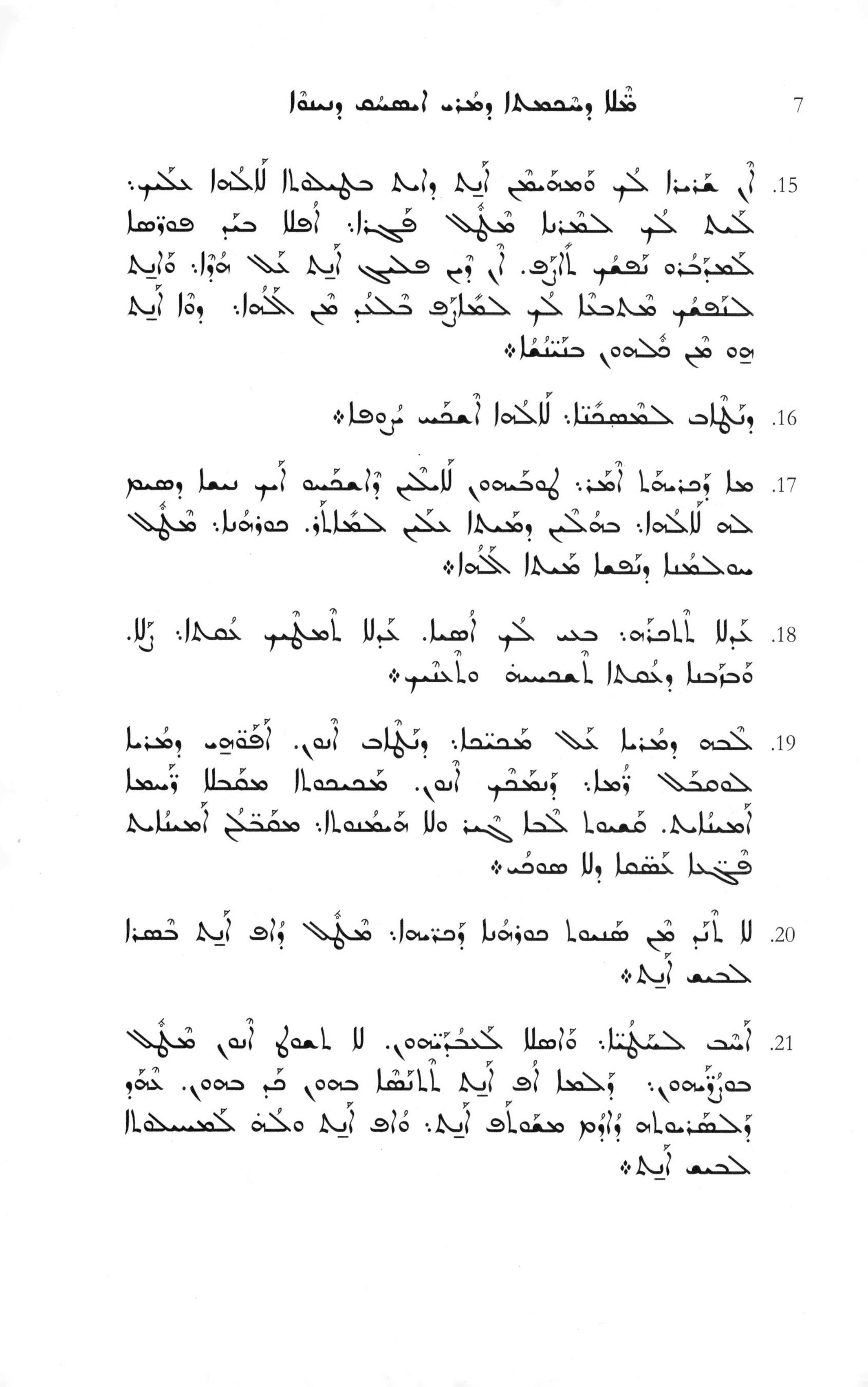

22. The knowledge of God does not reside in a body that loves comforts.

[Hom. 6, B 83]

23. Just as it is only after labour that a pregnant woman give birth to the fruit that gives joy, so it is with the soul: only after labours is knowledge of the mysteries of God given birth in it.

[Hom. 6, B 83]

24. There are people who are continually making clever plans, but who never get down to beginning on them.

[Hom. 6, B 96]

25. Commence every good action wholeheartedly. Do not approach it "with two hearts" (Ben Sira 1:28). As you travel through life, do not let your heart doubt about the hope that God's grace provides, otherwise your toil will be in vain and the labour of your work will weigh heavily upon you. Rather, have faith in your heart that God is compassionate, and to those who ask Him He gives His grace—not in accord with our work, but corresponding to the love in our souls and our faith in Him. "As you have believed, so it shall be to you" (Matthew 9:29).

[Hom. 6, B 97]

26. Begin on every action that is for God's sake joyfully.

[Hom. 6, B 98]

27. Just as the sun's rays are sometimes hidden from the earth by thick cloud, so for a while a person may be deprived of spiritual comfort and of grace's brightness: this is caused by the cloud of the passions. Then, all of a sudden, without that person being aware, it is all given back. Just as the surface of the earth rejoices at the rays of the sun when they break through the clouds, so the words of prayer are able to break through to drive the thick cloud of the passions away from the soul.

[Hom. 13, B 124]

28. Constant pondering on the holy Scriptures will always fill the soul with incomprehensible wonder and joy in God.

[Hom. 13, B 125]

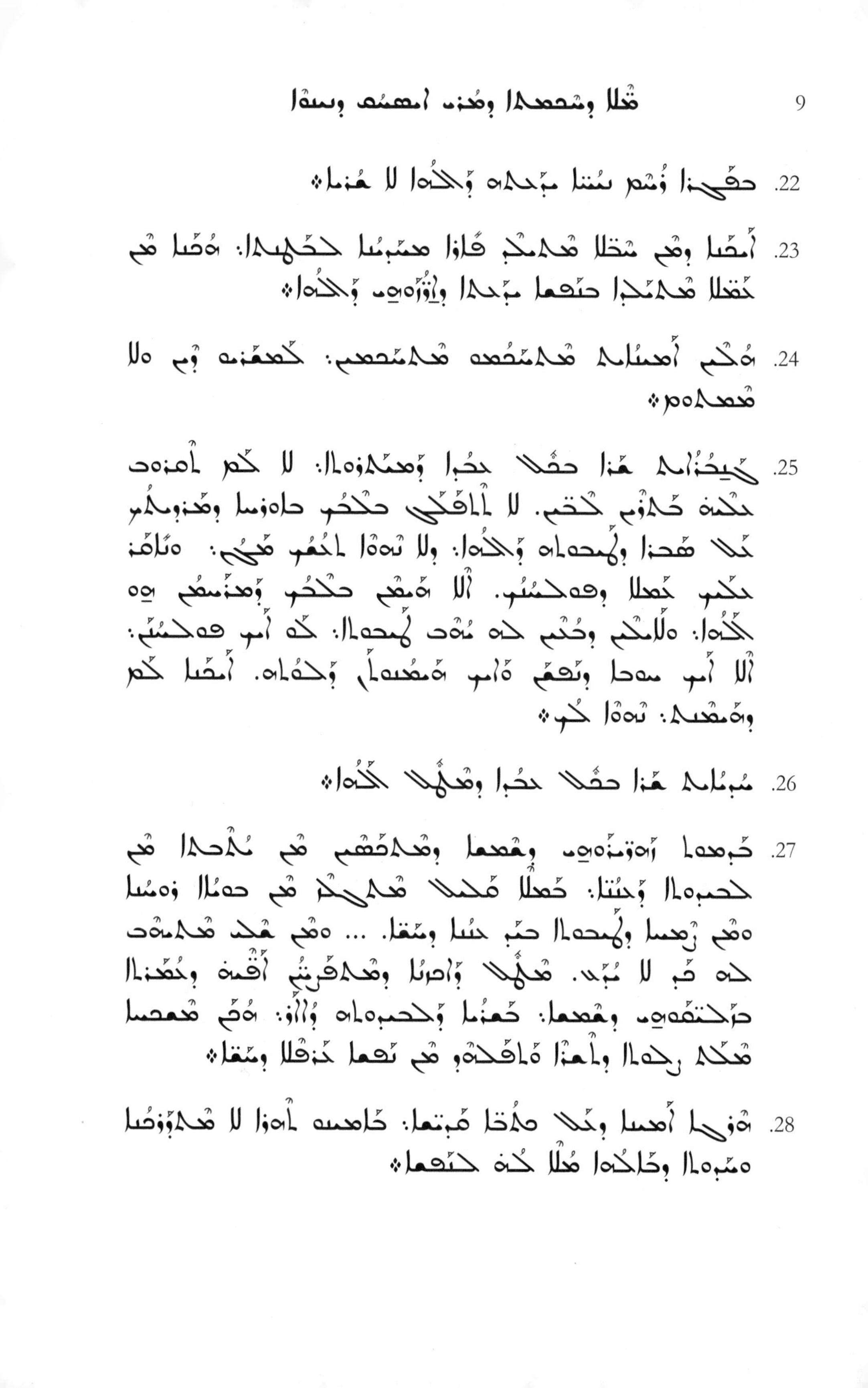

29. Every prayer over which the body does not share the toil, and over which the heart does not feel suffering, you should consider to be stillborn.

[Hom. 18, B 144]

30. Nothing, whether it be good or bad, happens to a person by blind chance. There is a provident God who steers the affairs of this world, and with each one of us there is a Guardian who does not miss anything, and whose watchfulness never relaxes or grows weak.

[Hom. 23, B 176]

31. God is compassionate, and He loves to give, but He wants us to be the reason for His giving. Thus His delight is when someone offers up to Him a wise prayer.

[Hom. 24, B 181]

32. 'Satan' is a name denoting the deviation of the human will from truth; it is not the designation of a natural being.

[Hom. 26, B 189]

33. A farmer gets pleasure from bread that is produced as a result of the sweat of his labour. Until one first sweats, the True Bread does not give satisfaction.

[Hom. 26, B 191]

34. The suffering that grips the heart as a result of sinning against love is sharper than all other tortures.

[Hom. 27, B 201]

35. A little endurance in face of small matters will hold back danger when serious ones come; for it is not possible to overcome great evils without a small victory over trifling matters.

[Hom. 30, B 214]

36. The intellect will not be glorified with Jesus unless the body suffers for the sake of Jesus.

[Hom. 34, B 222]

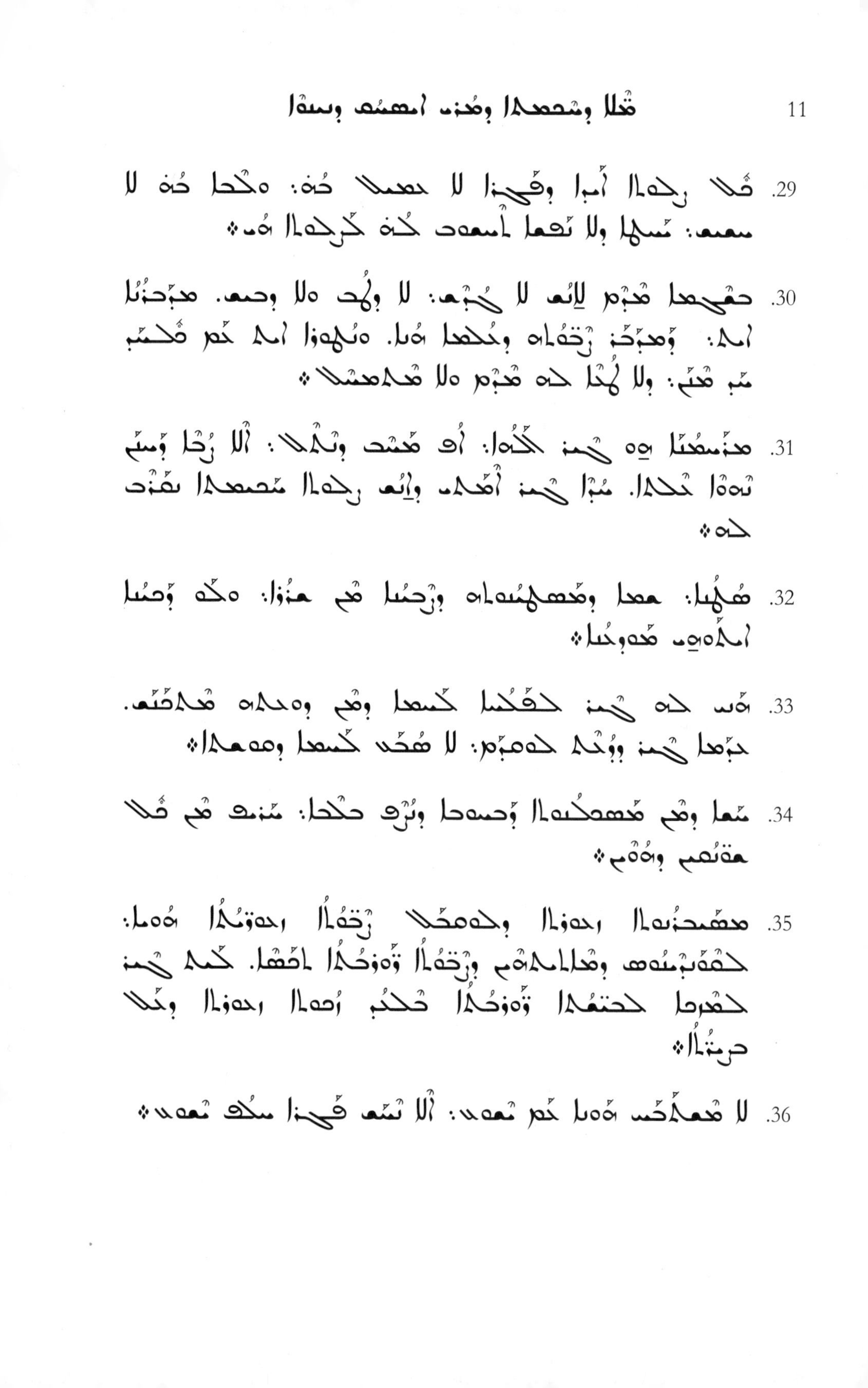

37. Courageousness of heart, and scorning every danger, come from one
     of two causes: either they are due to hardness of heart, or from an
     abundant faith in God. The former is accompanied by pride, the latter
     by humility of heart.

[Hom. 38, B 291]

38. It is a hard thing to be a slave serving the body.

[Hom. 38, B 291]

39. Virtue does not consist in many different visible bodily activities, but
     in a heart that is wise in what it hopes for, and whose actions are
     accompanied by a right intention.

[Hom. 38, B 292]

40. Faith is the gate to the mysteries. What the body's eyes are in relation
     to perceptible objects, so it is with faith in the case of the treasures that
     lie hidden to the eyes of the mind.

[Hom. 43, B 315]

41. When we have found love, we eat the Heavenly Bread, and receive
     nourishment without labour of weariness. The heavenly Bread is He
     who came down from heaven and gives life to the world (cf. John
     6:33). This is the Food of angels (Psalm 78:25). He who has found
     love, consumes Christ at all times, and becomes immortal from then
     on.

[Hom. 43, B 316]

42. Blessed is the person who has eaten of the Bread of love, which is
     Jesus.

[Hom. 43, B 316-7]

43. As we cross the sea of the world repentance should be our ship,
     reverential awe its pilot, while love is the divine harbour.

[Hom. 43, B 317]

44. The person who has attained to knowledge of his own weakness has
     reached the summit of humility.

[Hom. 45, B 321]

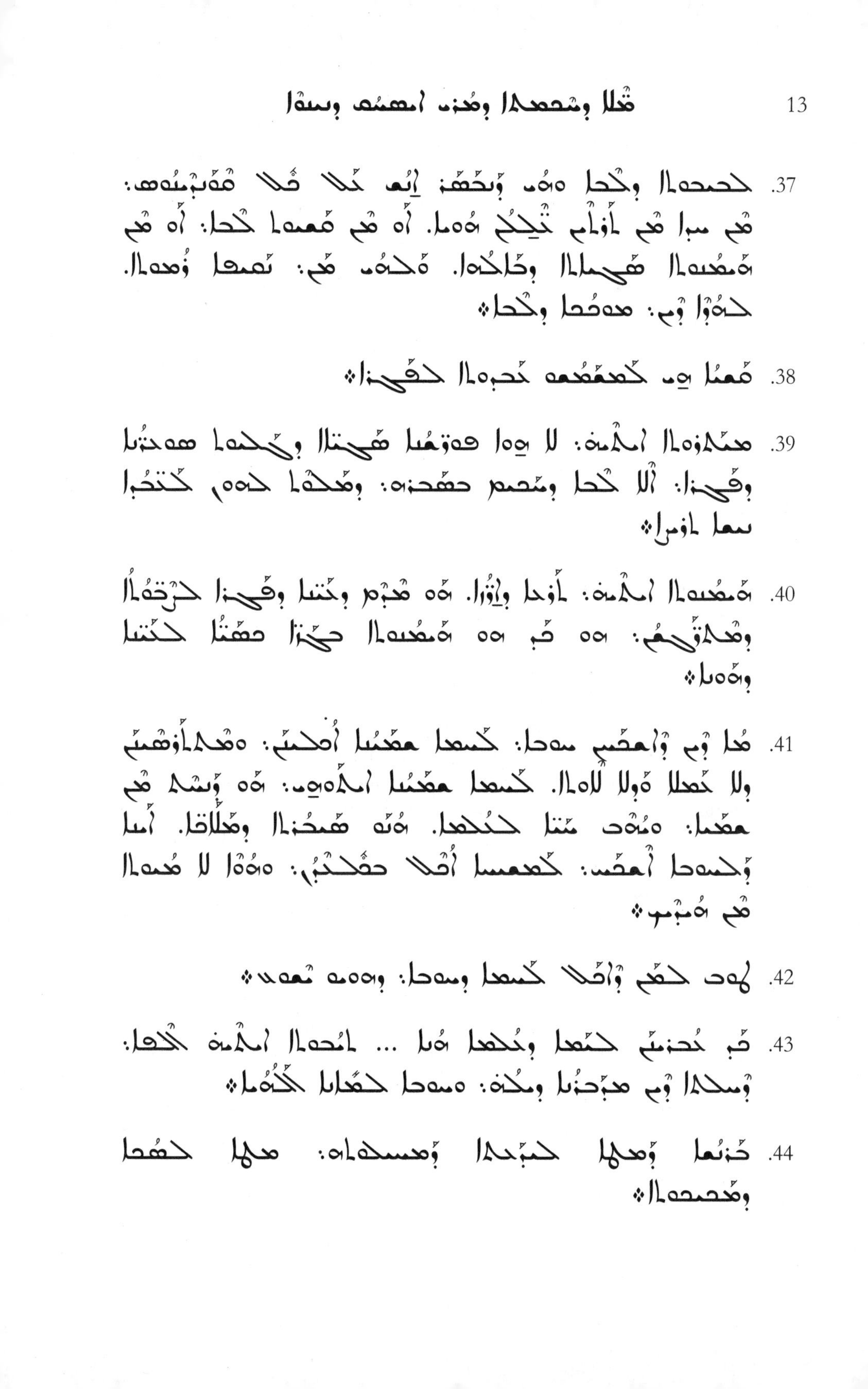

45. The mouth which is continuously giving thanks receives blessing from God. In the heart that always shows gratitude, grace abides.

[Hom. 45, B 322]

46. A righteous person who is wise resembles God; he never disciplines anyone in order to take vengeance on a wrongdoing, but only so that the person may be set aright, or that others may be deterred.

[Hom. 45, B 323]

47. The mind that has discovered spiritual wisdom is like a person who has found, in the midst of the sea, a well-equipped boat: when he gets aboard it, it conveys him from the sea of this world and brings him to the isle of the world to come.

[Hom. 45, B 325]

48. A cloud covers over the sun, and much discourse covers over the soul that has begun to receive illumination in contemplative prayer.

[Hom. 45, B 326]

49. Unripe fruits on trees are sour and disagreeable to the taste, and they are not suitable for eating until they acquire sweetness from the sun. Likewise the first labours of repentance are bitter and very disagreeable, and they do not give the Solitary any comfort until they acquire the sweetness that comes from contemplation.

[Hom. 45, B 328]

50. A small cloud can cover over the sun's orb, but the sun that follows it shines all the brighter. A little dejection can cover over the soul, but the joy that follows it is all the more filled with delight.

[Hom. 45, B 328]

51. Do not approach the mystery-filled words of the Scriptures without prayer and a request for assistance from God. Say, "Lord, grant me to become aware of the power in the words". Consider prayer to be the key to insights into Truth in the Scriptures.

[Hom. 45, B 329]

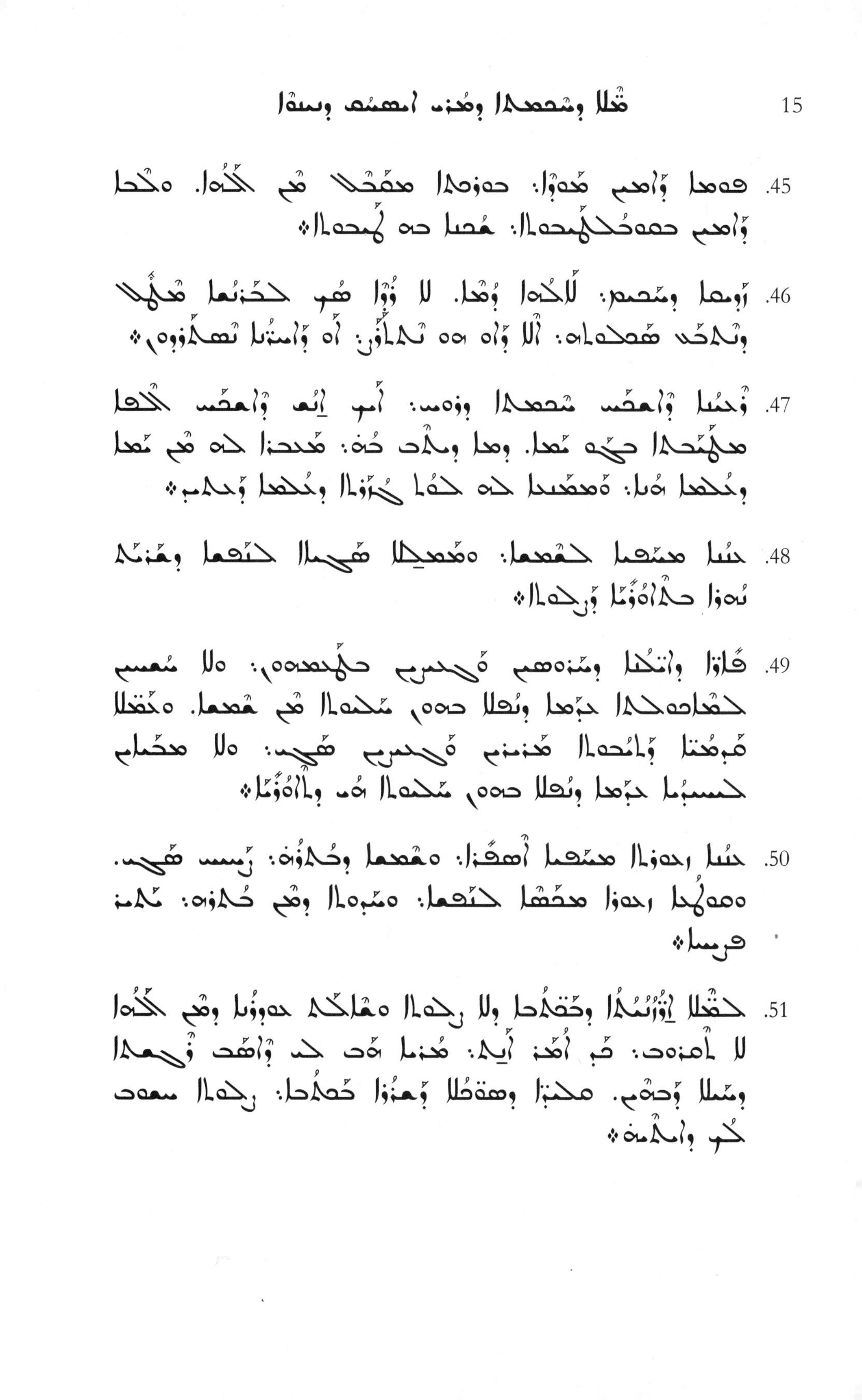

52. A key to God's gifts is given to the heart by means of love of one's neighbour.

[Hom. 46, B 330]

53. Ease and idleness effect the destruction of souls.

[Hom. 46, B 333]

54. When the soul is inebriated with joy at the object of its hope, and with exultation in God, then the body will no longer be aware of afflictions, even though it is brought very low.

[Hom. 46, B 333-4]

55. Even if you do not possess a pure heart, at least let your speech be pure.

[Hom. 46, B 334]

56. The more a person enters the struggle for the sake of God, the closer will his heart come to freedom of converse in prayer.

[Hom. 46, B 335]

57. We should not be upset at times when we are in darkness; this is especially important if we are not the cause of that darkness, for God's care is effecting this, for reasons of which He alone is aware.

[Hom. 48, B 339]

58. At the time of darkness, more than anything else kneeling is helpful.

[Hom. 49, B 341]

59. Even if our feelings are cold and dark, we should persevere in kneeling; even though our heart is dead at such times, and we cannot even pray, and do not know what to say since no words of prayer or supplication come to us, nevertheless we should continue to remain prostrate on our faces, even though we are silent.

[Hom. 49, B 341]

60. Just as a grain of sand will not balance in the scales against a great weight of gold, such too is the case with God's justice when it is weighed against His compassion. When compared with God's mind, the sins of all flesh are like a handful of sand thrown in the sea.

[Hom. 50, B 345]

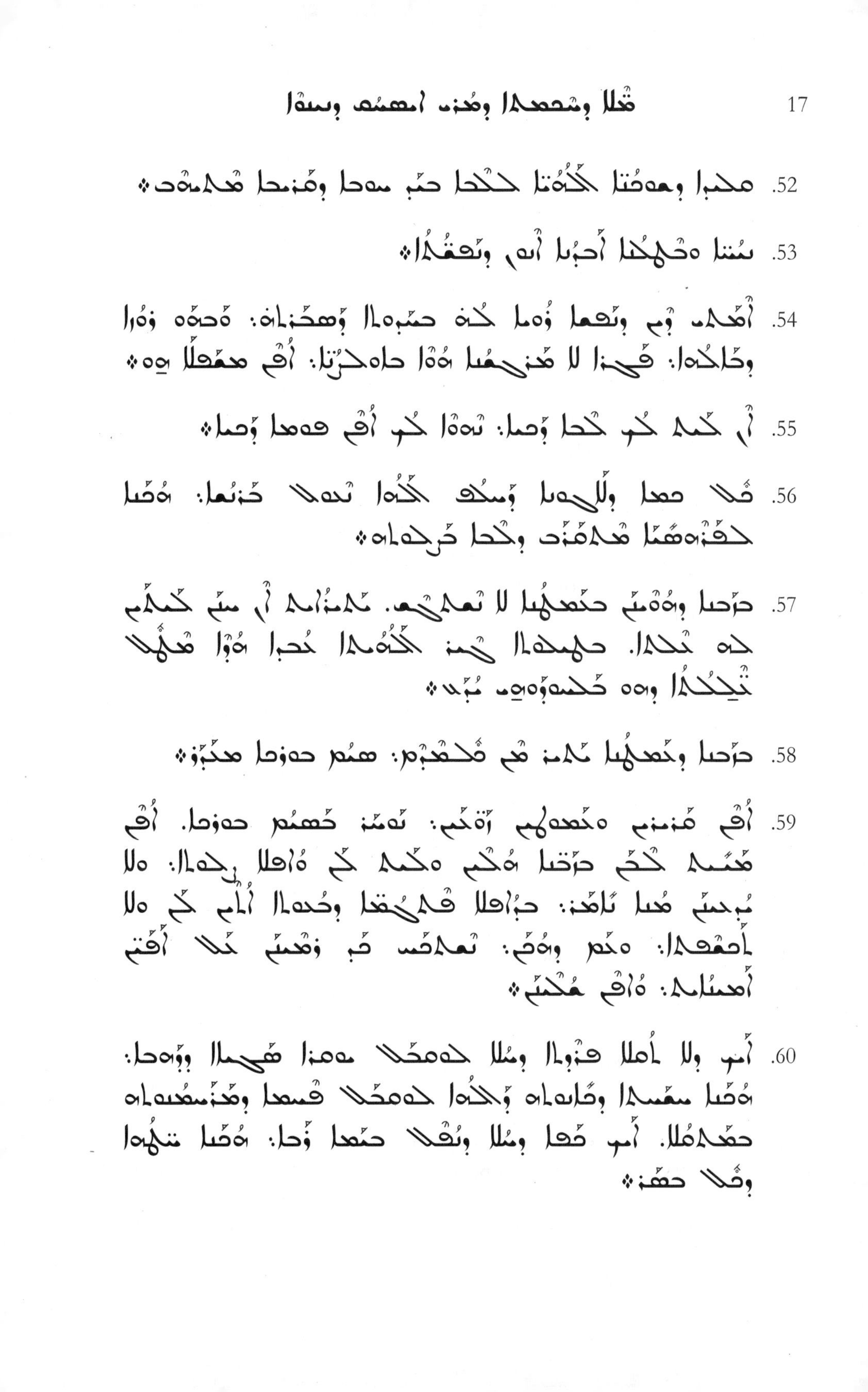

61. Just as an abundantly flowing fountain is not blocked by a handful of dust, so the Maker's mercy is not overcome by the wickedness of those whom He has created.

[Hom. 50, B 345]

62. If you give something to someone in need, let a smile, together with kind words and encouragement in their suffering, precede your giving.

[Hom. 50, B 348]

63. The day you open your mouth to denigrate somebody, consider yourself as dead to God and emptied of all your labours.

[Hom. 50, B 348]

64. Remember that Christ died for the wicked, as Scripture says (Romans 5:6), and not for the good. Consider it a much greater thing to suffer on behalf of evil people and to do good to sinners, than to do this for the righteous.

[Hom. 50, B 348]

65. Rebuke that starts out from envy is a poisoned arrow.

[Hom. 50, B 349]

66. Be someone persecuted rather than become a persecutor.

[Hom. 50, B 349]

67. Prefer to be treated unjustly yourself to treating someone else in an unjust way.

[Hom. 50, B 349]

68. Rejoice with those who rejoice, and weep with those who weep, for this is a sign of serenity.

[Hom. 50, B 349-50]

69. Even if you are not a peace-maker, at least do not be a trouble-maker.

[Hom. 50, B 351]

70. If you have no means of stopping up the mouth of the person who denigrates his fellow human being, at least be on your guard yourself, lest you become his partner.

[Hom. 50, B 351]

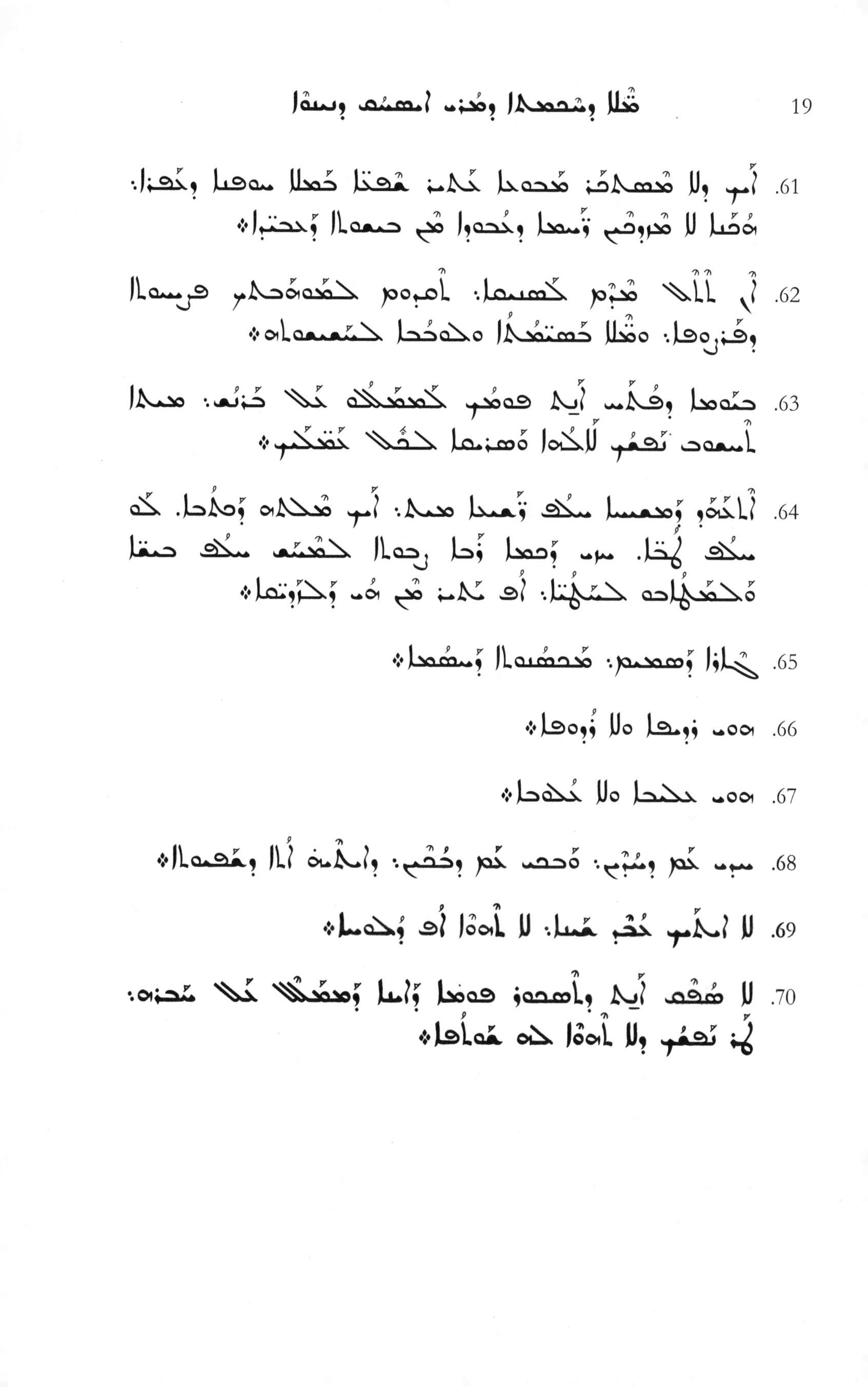

71. Undistracted prayer is prayer which produces the continual thought of God in the soul.

[Hom. 50, B 353]

72. We should not be unduly upset if we slip up in some matter: this is only a cause for concern when we continue to do so.

[Hom. 50, B 355]

73. Do not hate the sinner, for we are all guilty. If it is for the sake of God that you feel moved, then weep for that person; why should you hate him? Or perhaps, if it is his sins you are hating, then pray for that person, so that you may imitate Christ who never got angry with sinners, but prayed for them.

[Hom. 50, B 356]

74. Be a herald of God's grace, seeing that He provides you with His grace, even though you are not worthy of it.

[Hom. 50, B 357]

75. Knowledge is a step on the ladder up to faith. Once someone has reached faith, he does not need to use knowledge any longer.

[Hom. 51, B 367]

76. Even government treasuries of earthly powers do not refrain from taking a small coin from a beggar in order to increase their holdings: out of small trickles, there grow up mighty streams of great rivers.

[Hom. 53, B 380]

77. The way to God consists in a daily cross (cp. John 16:33): no one can ascend to heaven in comfort—we know where the road of comfort leads to!

[Hom. 59, B 417-8]

78. The desire of the Spirit for those in whom the Spirit dwells is not to let them grow accustomed to laziness, or to invite them to a life of ease, but rather to one of labours and much affliction. Accordingly the Spirit teaches them wakefulness, strengthens them in trials, and brings them to wisdom.

[Hom. 60, B 423]

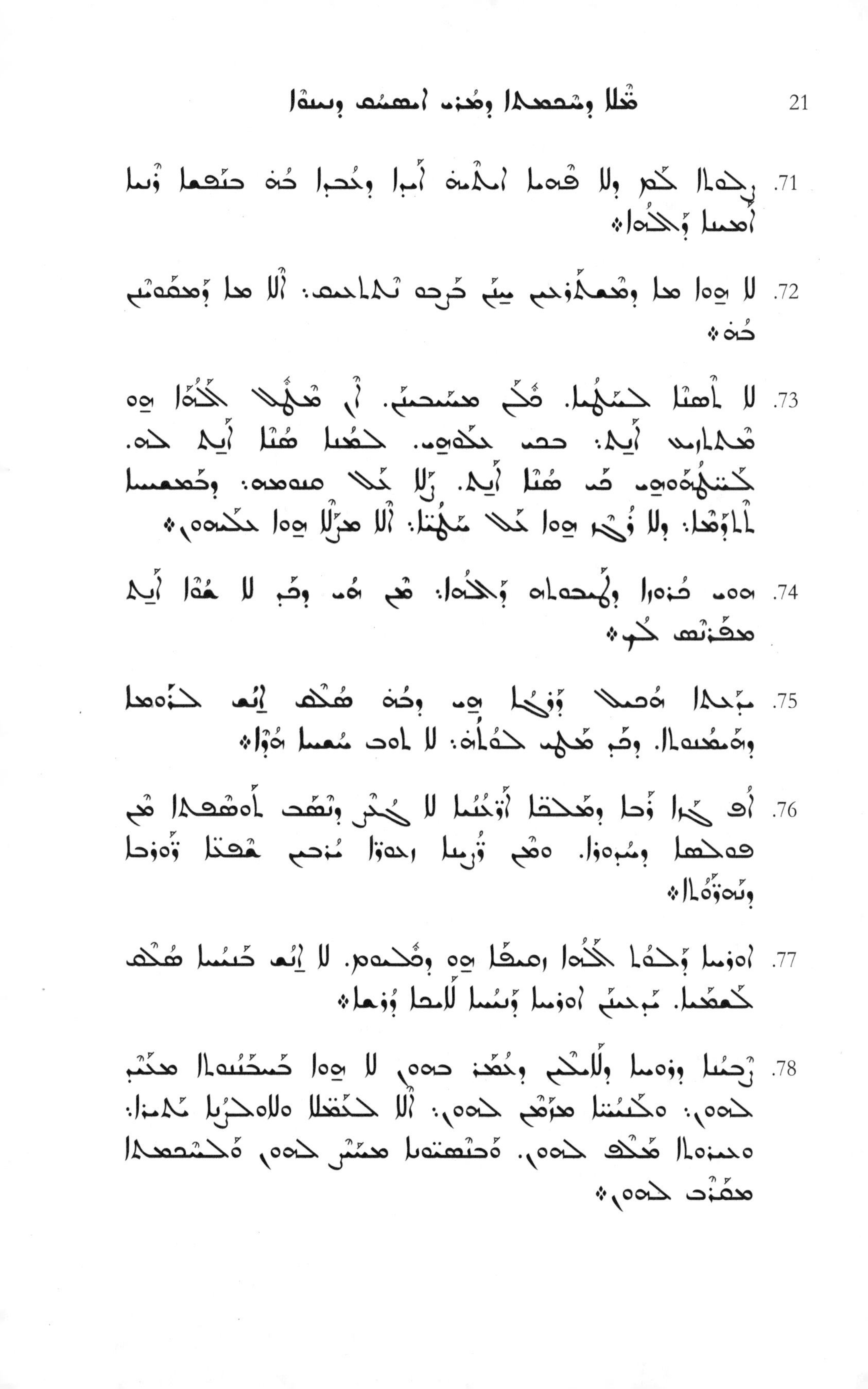

79. A time of trial is beneficial to everyone: the diligent are tried so that their wealth may increase; the lax, so that they may be preserved from harm; those spiritually asleep, so that they may prepare themselves for watchfulness; those who are far from God, so that they approach Him; those who are God's close associates, so that they may come closer to Him in freedom of speech.

[Hom. 61, B 429]

80. Love is sweeter than life; but even sweeter than honey and a honeycomb is an insight concerning God out of which love is born.

[Hom. 62, B 431]

81. Our way of life in this world resembles a document that is still in draft form: things can be added or taken out, and alterations can be made, whenever one wants. But life in the world to come resembles the case of completed documents that have the king's seal already upon them, and no addition or subtraction can be made. While we are still here, where changes can be made, let us take a look at ourselves, and while we still have control over the book of our life, and it is in our hands, let us be eager to add to it by means of a good life-style, and delete from it the defects of our former life-style.

[Hom. 62, B 436]

82. The aim of prayer is so that we should acquire from it love of God, for in prayer are to be found all sorts of reasons for loving God.

[Hom. 63, B 439]

83. Repentance is able to renew within us the grace which we have lost, subsequent to baptism, through our lax way of life.

[Hom. 65, B 443]

84. You should be aware that not every book that gives instruction about the spiritual life is also useful for the purification of the conscience and the recollection of the thoughts.

[Hom. 65, B 447]

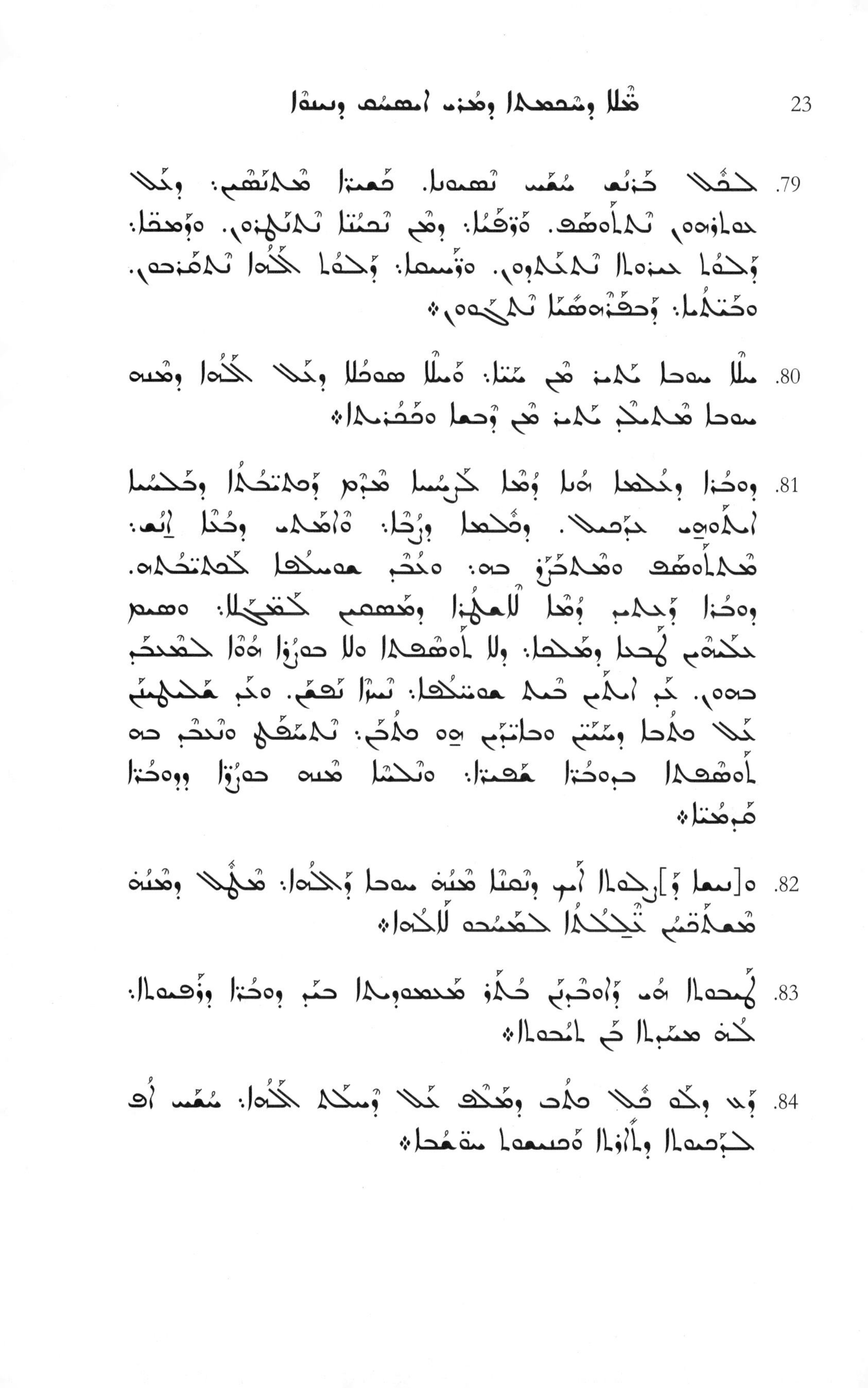

85. A compassionate person is the physician of his own soul, for, as if with a strong wind, he chases away from his inner being a dark cloud.

[Hom. 65, B 455]

86. Compassion is an excellent investment with God, for, according to the Gospel of Life, "Blessed are the compassionate, since upon them there shall be compassion" (Matthew 5:7).

[Hom. 65, B 455-6]

87. The following shall serve for you as a luminous sign of your soul's serenity: when, on examining yourself you find yourself filled with compassion for all humanity, and your heat is smitten with pity, and burns as if with fire, on behalf of everyone without distinction.

[Hom. 71, B 492]

88. Humility, even without ascetic labours, expiates many sins. Ascetic labours that are not accompanied by humility, however, are not only of no benefit, but they actually bring upon us much harm.

[Hom. 72, B 499]

89. As salt is needed for all kinds of food, so humility is needed for all kinds of virtues.

[Hom. 72, B 499]

90. Some people are robbed of their hope at the very gates of their home—that is to say, in old age.

[Hom. 79, B 543]

91. Someone who shows compassion to the afflicted is like a person who has a good advocate in the law courts.

[Hom. 79, B 544]

92. The more the sufferings of Christ abound in us, the greater will our consolation in Christ become.

[Hom. 79, B 544]

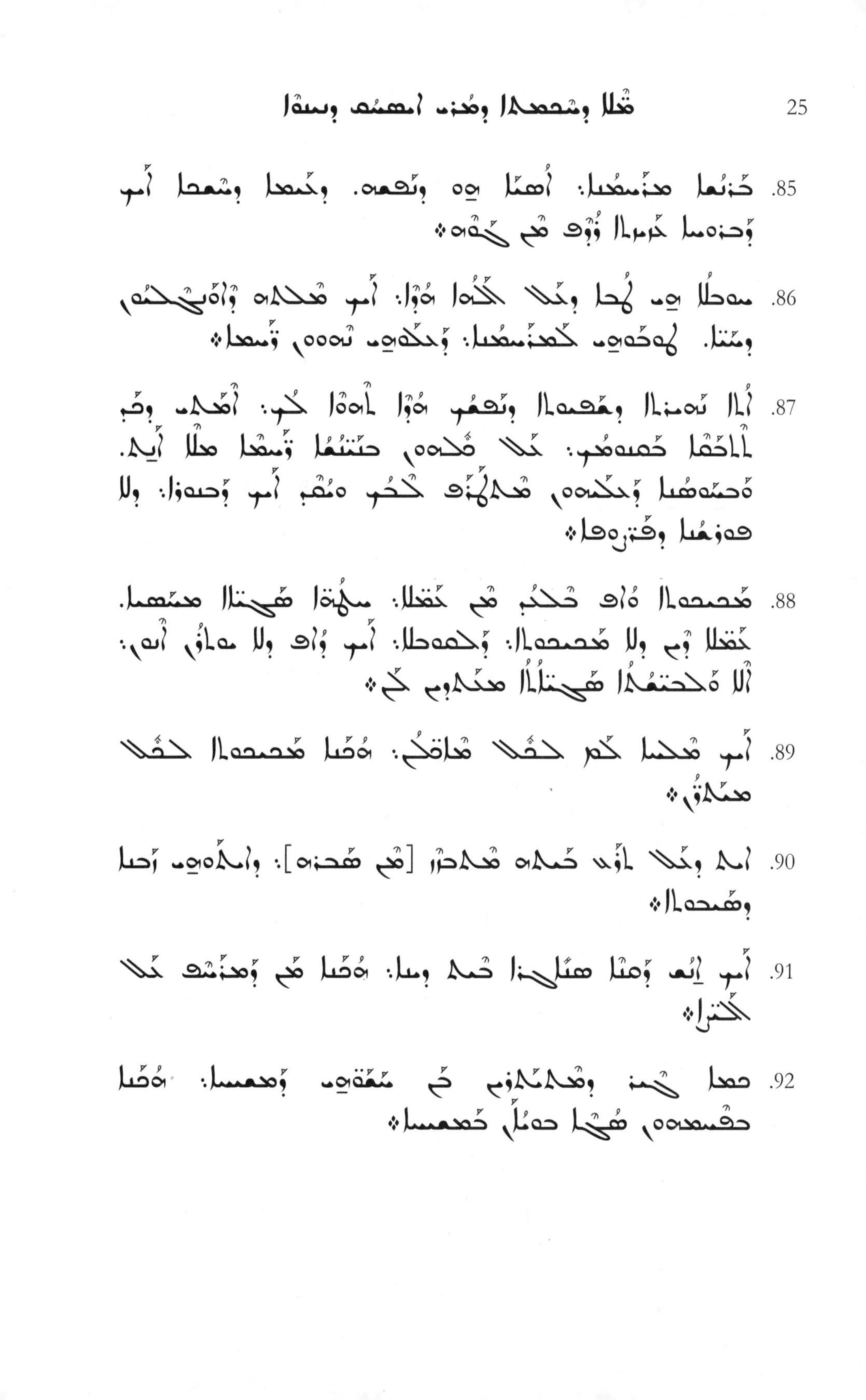

93. If you fall into temptations, do not despair, for there is not a single merchant travelling by sea or land, who does not suffer some loss, and there is not a single farmer who gathers in absolutely everything he has sown.

[Hom. 80, B 565]

94. Without love for our neighbour, the mind is not able to become illumined by means of converse with God and divine love.

[Hom. 81, B 567]

95. Humility is the robe of divinity: for when God the Word became incarnate He put on humility and thereby communicated with us by means of our human body. Accordingly, everyone who is truly clothed in humility will resemble Him who descended from the height, hiding the radiance of His greatness and covering up His glory by means of His low estate.

[Hom. 82, B 574].

96. A person receives illumination in accordance with the quality of his conduct before God.

[Keph. I.12].

97. Do not dispute over the truth with someone who does not know the truth; but from the person who is eager to know the truth, do not withhold words from him.

[Keph. I.14].

98. With a person who is unable to profit from spiritual knowledge, benefit him instead with your silence, rather than with words about such knowledge.

[Keph. I.15].

99. Do not consider a long time spent in worship before God to be wasted.

[Keph. I.20].

100. Those who just grab at knowledge are themselves grabbed by pride: the more they study, the more darkened they become.

[Keph. I.25].

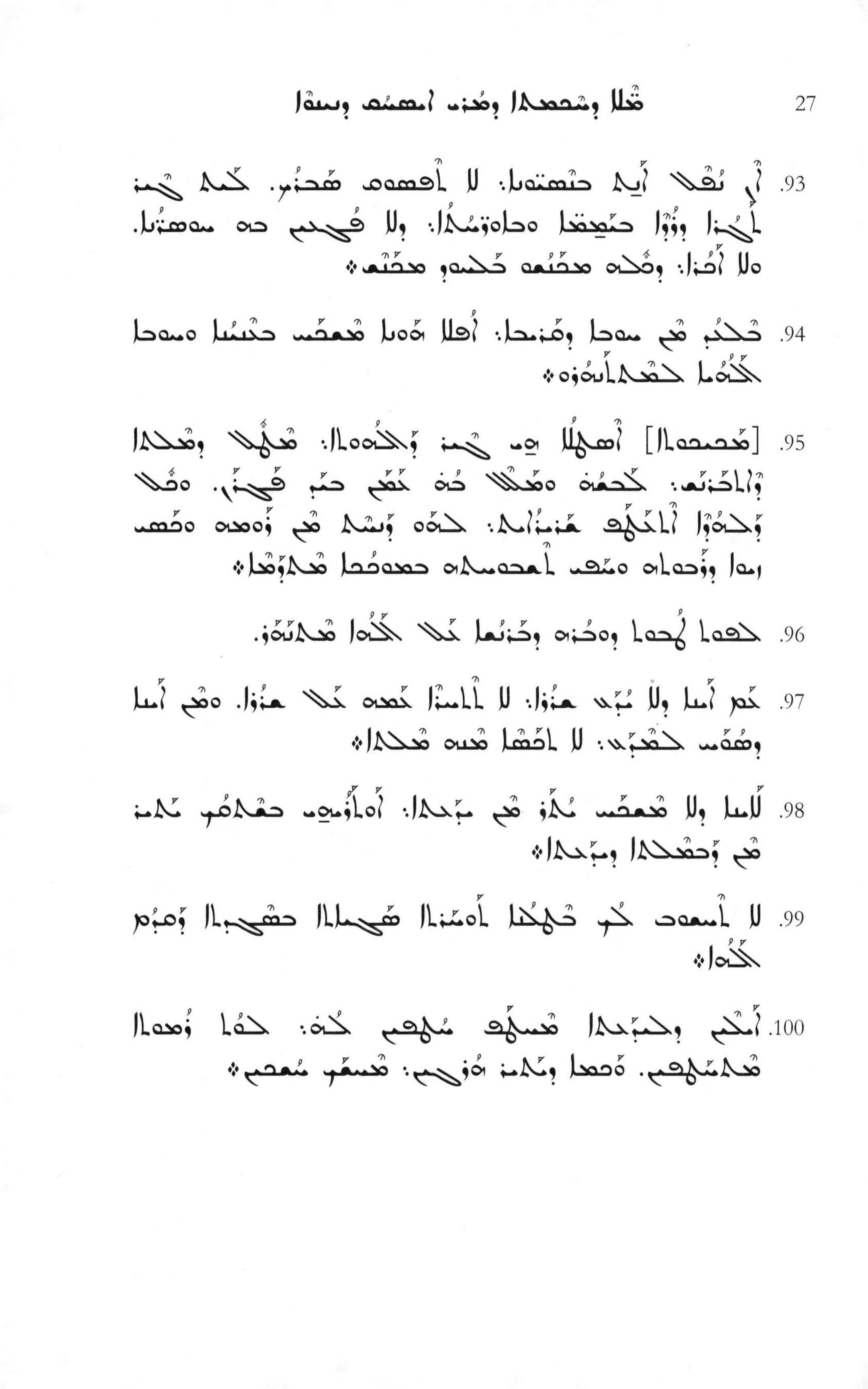

101. Those who rush at knowledge, without working for it, are the people who grab at it; in other words, instead of the truth, they grab at a semblance.

[Keph. I.26].

102. Whenever it is a time of battling with Satan and of darkness, one should spend extra time in prayer and in kneeling on the ground.

[Keph. I.30].

103. In the case of thoughts, we have the authority to bridle them—that is, if we are extremely alert; but over the body's functioning we do not have authority. Accordingly, anyone who says that he is without any passion when he fills his belly, or is continuously involved in material spectacles, has gone completely astray.

[Keph. I.31].

104. Impassibility does not consist in not being aware of the passions, but in not accepting the passions.

[Keph. I.33].

105. For someone to say to his brother "Love God" is very easy, but what is necessary is to know how to love Him.

[Keph. I.36].

106. Ease blinds a person so that he does not gaze upon divine matters with wonder; instead, it results in his examining them in an empty way.

[Keph. I.45].

107. What watering is to plants is exactly the same as continual silence for the growth of spiritual knowledge.

[Keph. I.47].

108. The person who loves labour is not someone who has no love for the comforts of the body, but someone who has no love for the concerns of the body.

[Keph. I.69]

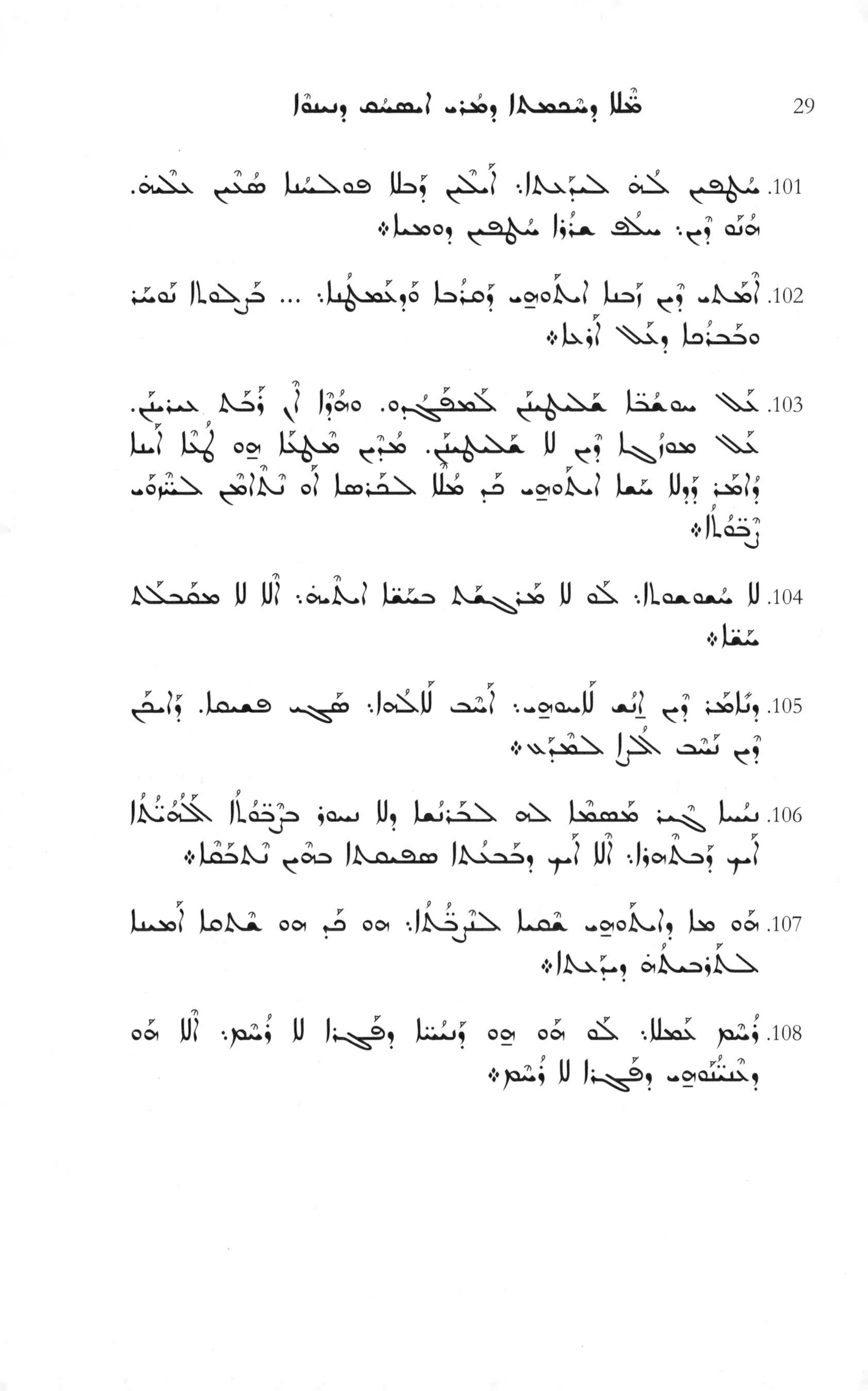

THE WISDOM OF ST ISAAC

109. Once the passions in the soul have been weakened and become silent through stillness, then a person can easily overcome the lusts of the body.

[Keph. I.70]

110. The person who loves praise is not someone who, when praised, feels pleasure at the praise, but the person who devises ways of getting praise.

[Keph. I.74]

111. The person who is humble in mind is someone whose mind, even when he is justly praised, takes no pleasure in this.

[Keph. I.75]

112. The soul's refuge in times of trials and sorrow is our Lord's own faith. The refuge for the soul's ministry is acknowledgement of its weakness.

[Keph. II.16]

113. Weakness of body does not hinder the yearning of a sound conscience from fulfilling the good, provided the will does not get lazy.

[Keph. II.82]

114. Suffering for the sake of God is a medicine for the person who is smitten with illness.

[Keph. II.99]

115. Prayer that is not accompanied by a good way of life is an eagle whose wings have been plucked.

[Keph. III.50]

116. Virtue is not the child of good actions, but of the good intention behind those actions.

[Keph. III.95]

117. Purity of prayer is silence from the chatter of thoughts about bodily matters.

[Keph. IV.32].

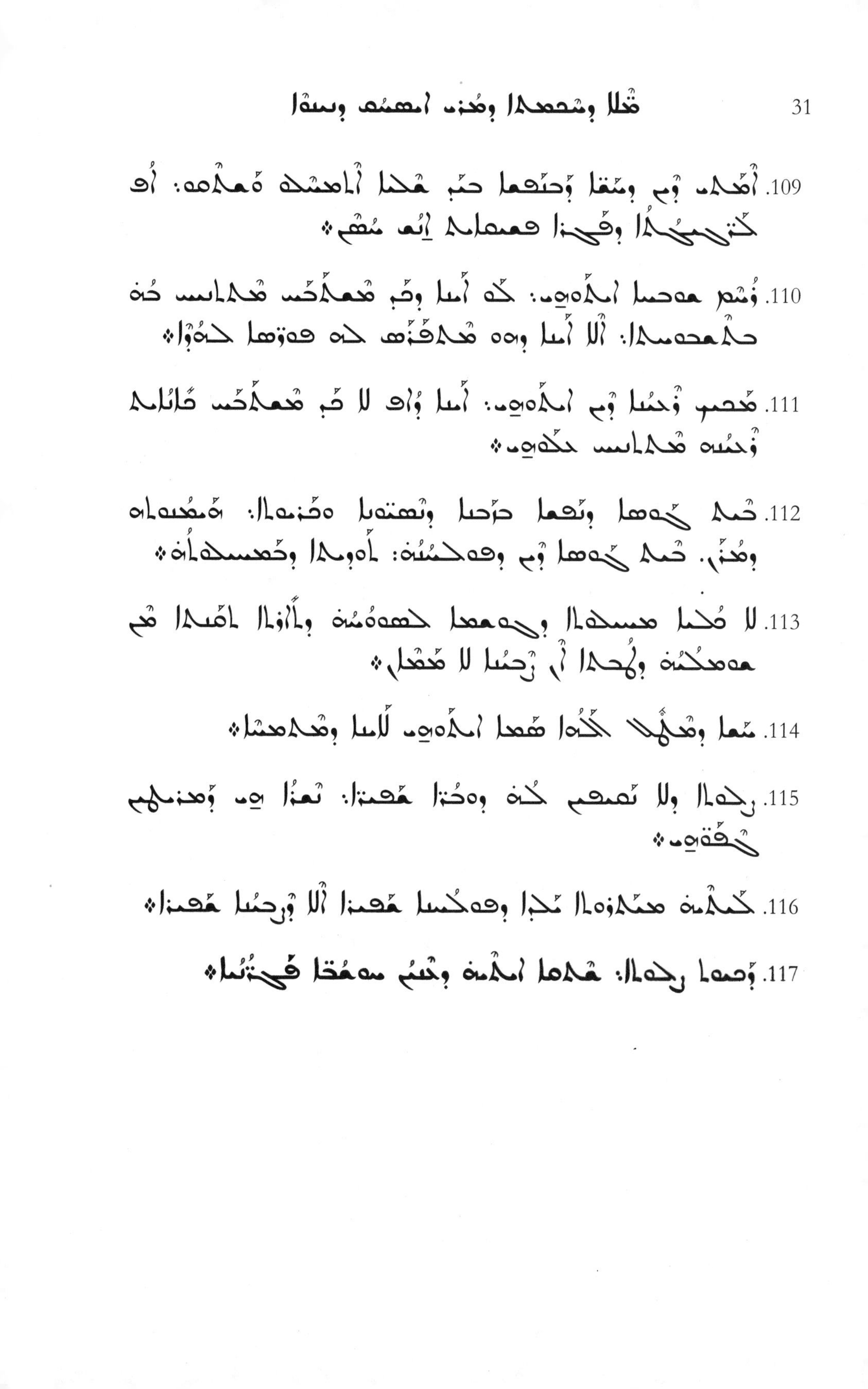

118. You should not wait until you are cleansed of wandering thoughts before you desire to pray. If you only begin on prayer when you see that your mind has become perfect and raised above all recollection of the world, then you will never pray.

[Keph. IV.34].

119. Someone who has actually tasted truth is not contentious for truth. Someone who is considered by people to be zealous for truth has not yet learnt what truth is really like; once he has truly learnt it, he will cease from zealousness on its behalf.

[Keph. IV.77].

120. The entire purpose of our Lord's death was not to redeem us from sins, or for any other reason, but solely in order that the world might become aware of the love which God has for creation. Had all this astounding affair taken place solely for the purpose of the forgiveness of sin, it would have been sufficient to redeem us by some other means. /

[Keph. IV.78].

121. Variation of different prayers greatly helps a mind which is harassed by distraction.

[IV.3]

122. Give yourself over to the labour of prayer and you will discover something which you cannot hear from another person.

[VI.6]

123. Purity of soul is the stripping away of the cares of the flesh and concern of thoughts about the body.

[VIII.3]

124. An infantile mind is one that entertains feeble conceptions about divine matters, having human ideas about them, which are inappropriate to God's majesty.

[VIII.9]

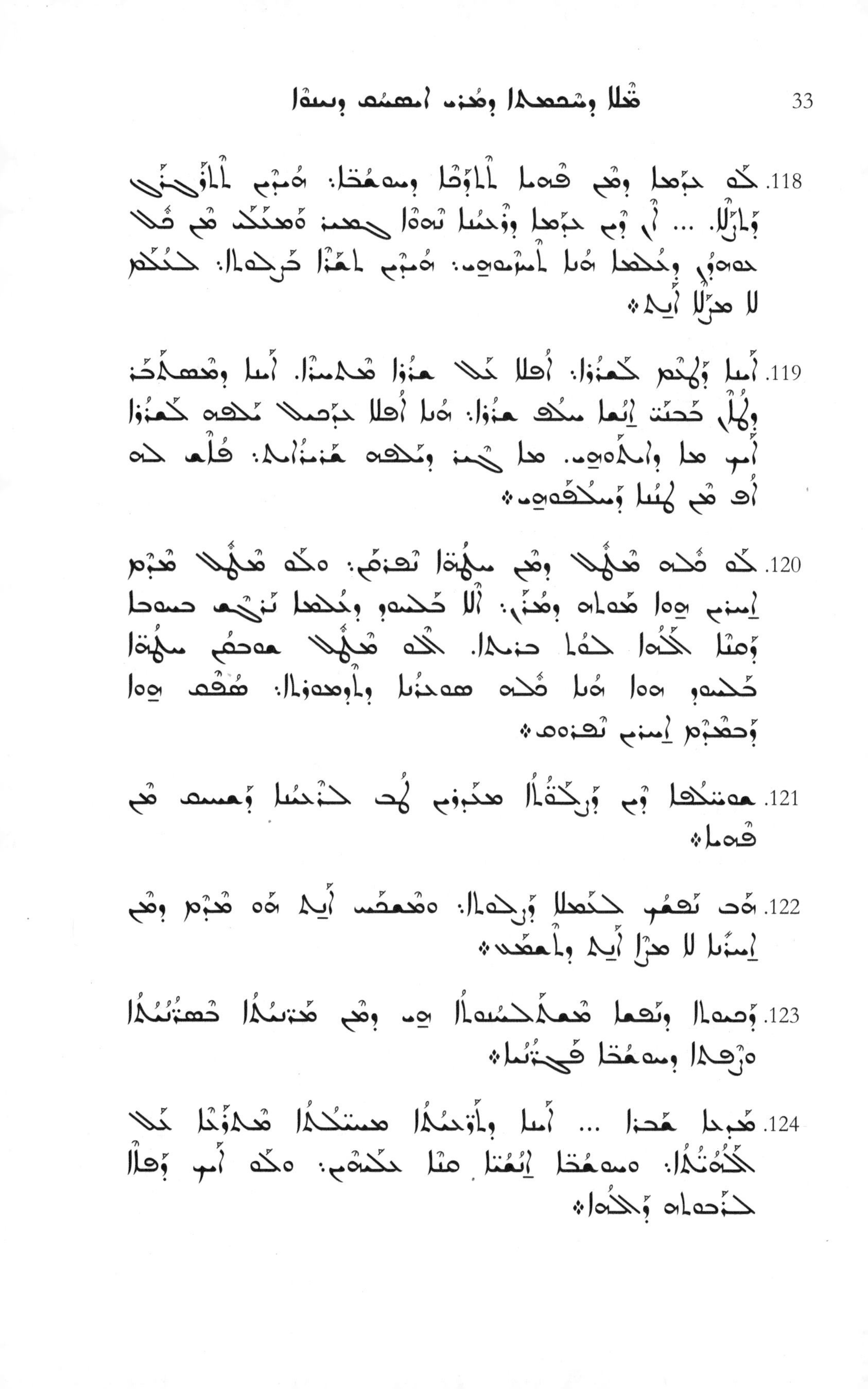

125. Do not try to make your course run more quickly than the divine Will wishes; do not be in such a hurry that you try to get ahead of the Providence which is guiding you—not that I am saying that you should not be eager.

[VIII.19]

126. For someone to entrust himself to God means that, from that point onwards, he will no longer be devoured by anguish or fear over anything; nor will he again be tormented by the thought that he has no one to look after him.

[VIII.21]

127. Once someone has doubted God's care for him, he immediately falls into a myriad of anxieties.

[VIII.26]

128. Anyone who fears sin will not fear Satan. And all who yearn for God's gift will have no dread of temptations. Anyone who believes firmly that the will of the Creator controls His entire creation will not be perturbed by anything.

[IX.1]

129. Knowledge of truth fills the heart with peace, establishing in a person joy and confidence.

[IX.2]

130. There is no virtue which does not have continual struggle yoked to it.

[X.13]

131. With the love of God a person will draw close to a perfect love of fellow human beings. No one has ever been able to draw close to this luminous love of humanity without having first been held worthy of the wonderful and inebriating love of God.

[X.33-34]

132. Blessed is God who continually uses corporeal objects to draw us close, in a mysterious way, to a knowledge of His invisible Being.

[XI.31]

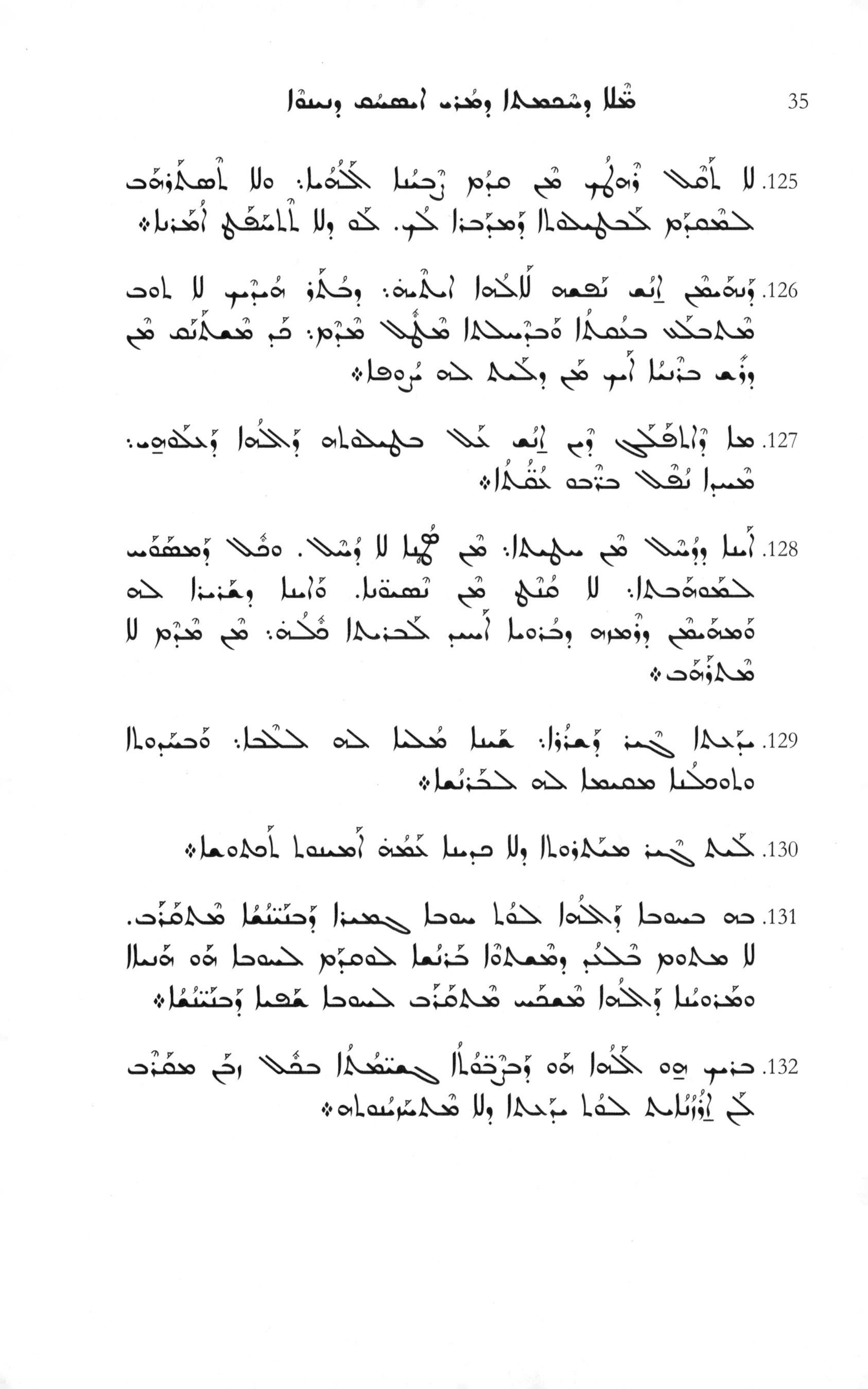

133. It is in proportion to the honour which someone shows in his person to God during the time of prayer—both with his body and with the mind—that the door of assistance will be opened for him, leading to the purifying of the impulses, and to illumination in prayer.

[XIV.11]

134. Someone who shows a reverential posture during prayer, by stretching out his hands to heaven as he stands in modesty, or by falling on his face to the ground, will be accounted worthy of much grace from on high as a result of these lowly actions.

[XIV.12]

135. God cannot be dishonoured by anything, seeing that honour belongs to Him by nature. But we, as a result of slovenly habits and various outward postures which lack reverence, have acquired an attitude of mind that shows contempt towards Him.

[XIV.13]

136. God accepts the paltry and insignificant things done with a good will for His sake, along with mighty and perfect actions.

[XIV.15]

137. The true vision of Jesus Christ our Lord consists in our realizing the meaning of His incarnation for our sakes, and becoming inebriated with love of Him as a result of the insights into the many wondrous elements contained in that vision.

[XIV.30]

138. May God make us worthy of a taste of His grace at all times, for by it we approach the wonder that surrounds Him

[XIV.48]

139. We should consider the labour of reading the Scriptures to be something extremely elevated, whose importance cannot be exaggerated. For it serves as the gate by which the intellect enters into the divine mysteries, and takes on strength for attaining to luminosity in prayer.

[XXI.13]

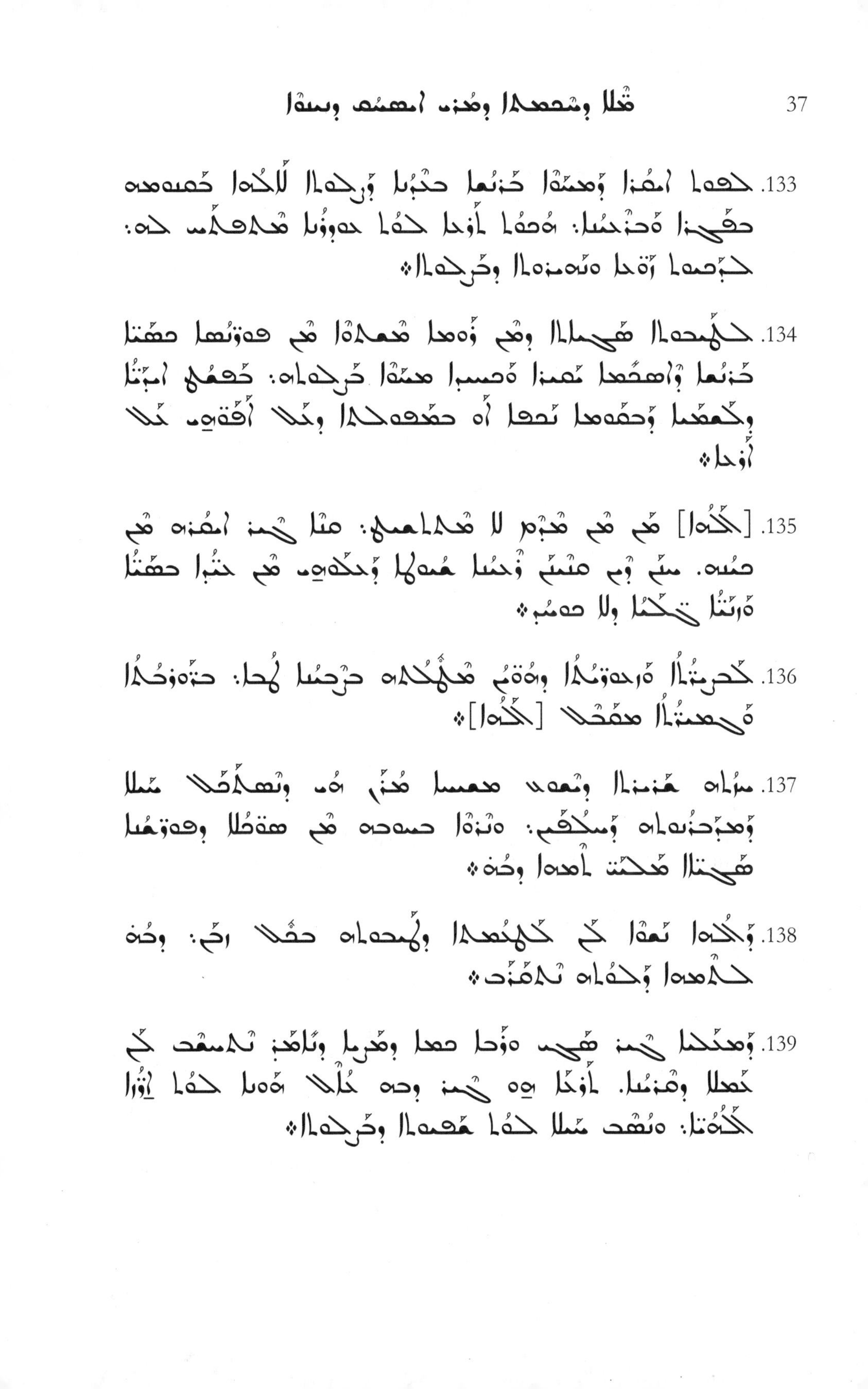

140. Truly, no bad event has a worse repayment than in the case of a foolish mind which is not willing to rebuke and blame itself.

[XXVI.6]

141. The reading of Scripture is manifestly the fountainhead which gives birth to prayer.

[XXIX.5].

142. It is a matter for great dread to approach God in a lax way, under the guise of freedom of speech, or on the pretext of liberty; for maybe all of a sudden some punishment may meet us at that point.

[XXXI.9]

143. If a diver found a pearl in every oyster, then everyone would quickly become rich.

[XXXIV.4]

144. In love did God bring the world into existence; in love does He guide it during its temporal existence; in love is He going to bring it to that wondrous transformed state, and in love will the world be swallowed up in the great mystery of Him who has performed all these things. In love will the whole course of the governance of creation be finally comprised.

[XXXVIII.2]

145. Just because the terms 'wrath', 'anger', 'hatred' and the rest are used of the Creator in the Bible, we should not imagine that He actually does anything in anger, hatred or zeal. Many figurative terms are used of God in the Scriptures, terms which are far removed from His true nature.

[XXXIX.19]

146. Among all God's actions there is none which is not entirely a matter of mercy, love and compassion: this constitutes the beginning and end of His dealings with us.

[XXXIX.22]

147. God's love is not a kind of love which has its origin in events which take place in time.

[XL.2].

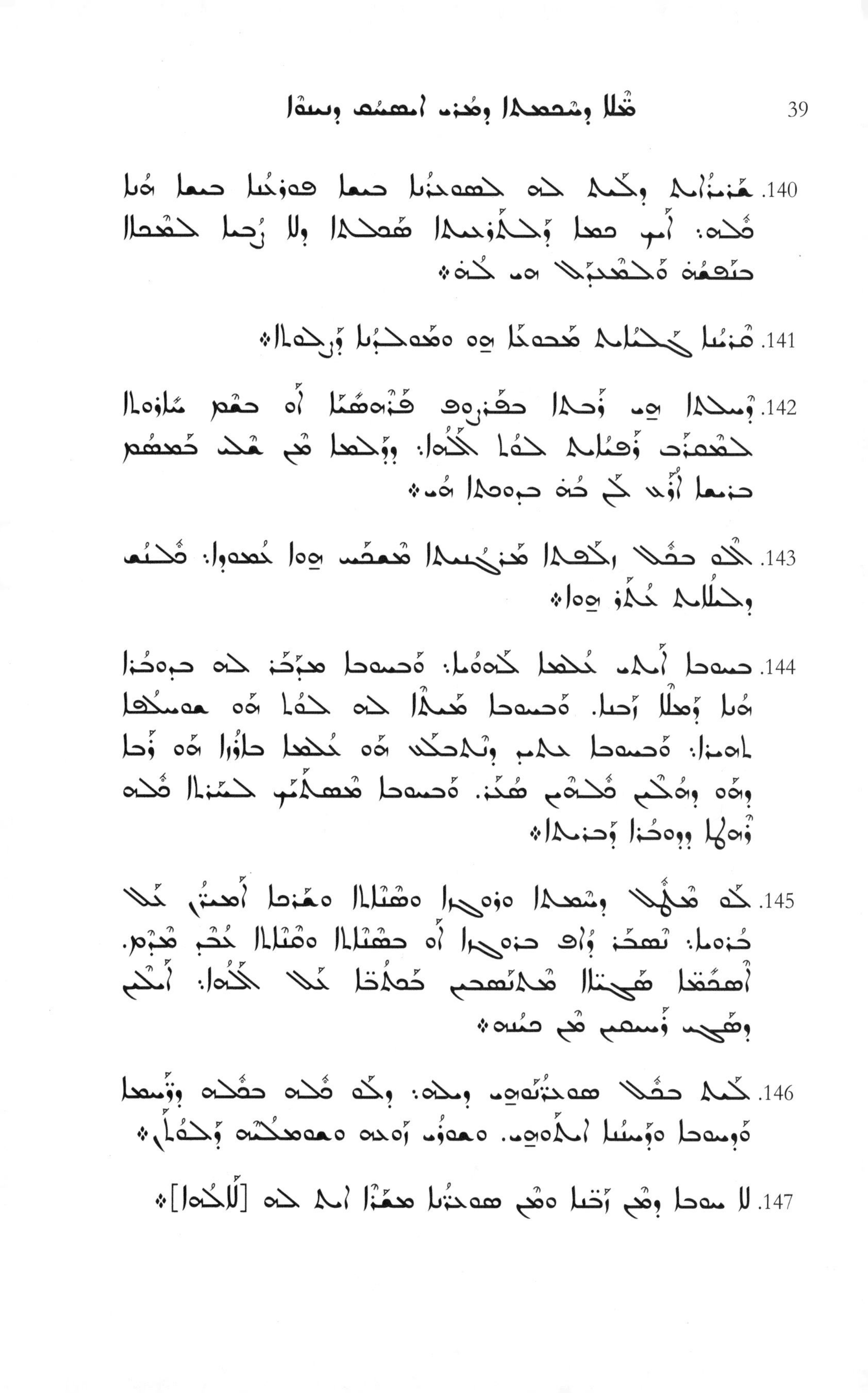

148. God has a single caring concern for those who have fallen, just as
     much as for those who have not fallen.

[XL.3].

149. It is God's wish that each day we should be renewed and start up again
     with a virtuous change of will, and with a renewal of mind.

[XL.9]

150. God's holy nature is so good and compassionate that it is always
     seeking to find some small means of setting us right.

[XL.12]

151. God's mercifulness is far more extensive than we can conceive.

[XL.17]

152. On the subject of God, it is right that only someone worthy of God
     because of his virtue should speak.

[XLI.1]

153. In your heart act as a priest to God, offering up a pure sacrifice.

[XLI.2]

*

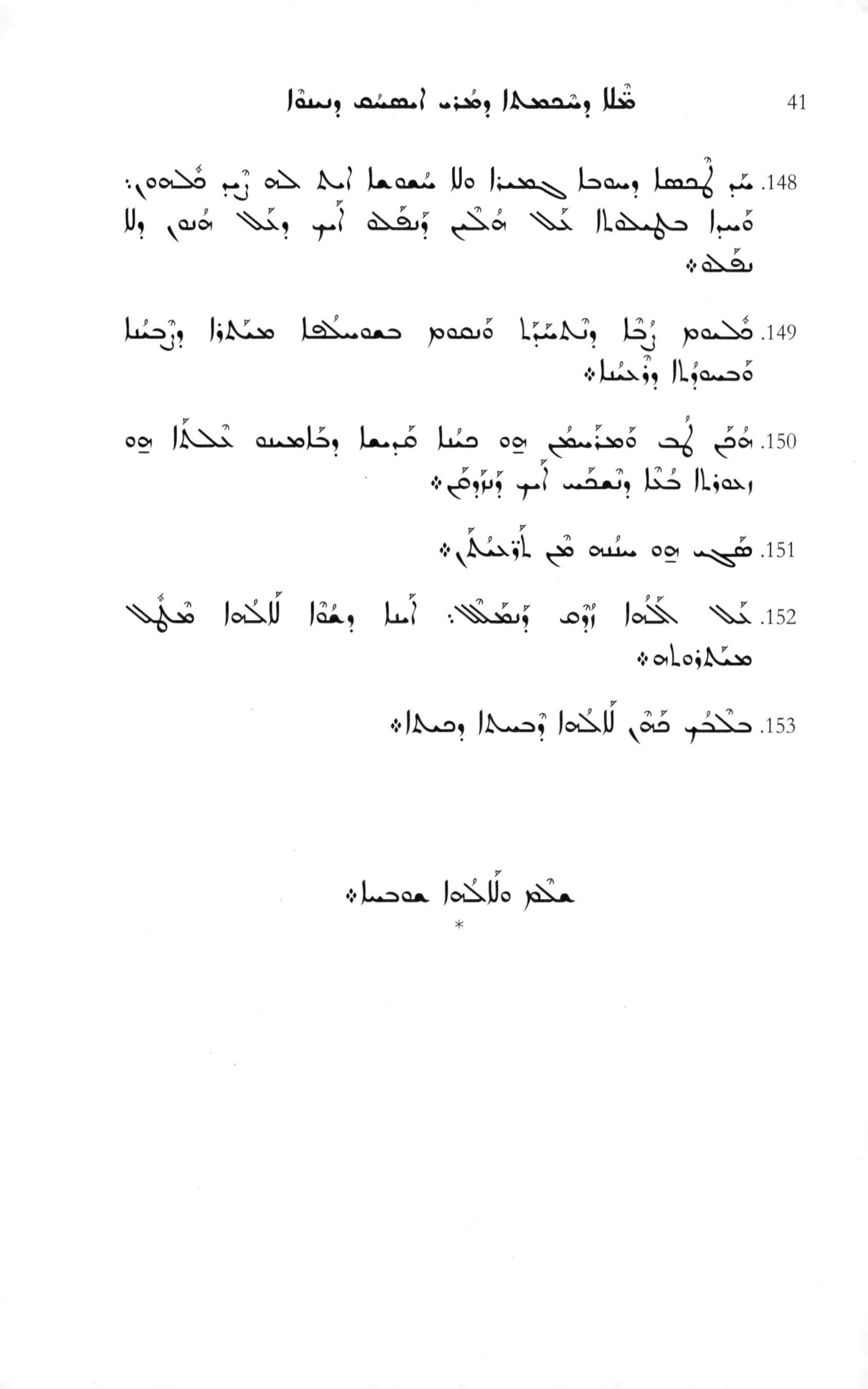

INDEX OF SUBJECTS